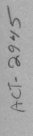

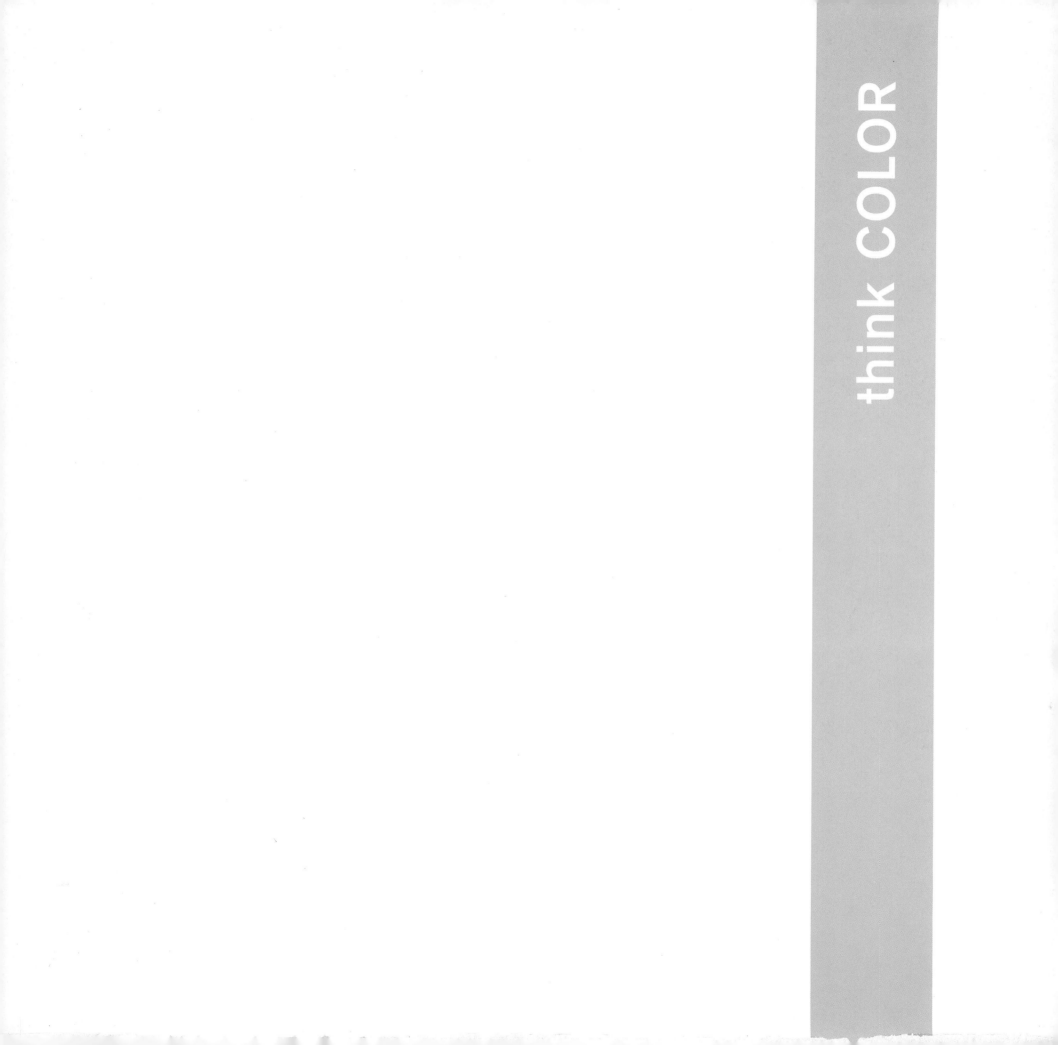

think COLOR

think COLOR

rooms to live in

by TRICIA GUILD

text by ELSPETH THOMPSON
with TRICIA GUILD
photographs by JAMES MERRELL

CHRONICLE BOOKS
SAN FRANCISCO

First published in the United States in 2003
by Chronicle Books LLC.

Photographs copyright © 2002 by James Merrell
Text copyright © 2002 by Elspeth Thompson

Library of Congress Cataloging-in-Publication
Data available.

ISBN: 0-8118-3670-3

Manufactured in Italy

Distributed in Canada by Raincoast Books
9050 Shaughnessy Street
Vancouver, British Columbia V6P 6E5

10 9 8 7 6 5 4 3 2 1

Chronicle Books LLC
85 Second Street
San Francisco, California 94105

www.chroniclebooks.com

contents

5 introduction

8 joyful vivacious mandarin citrus cerise

34 pure serene mauve sea green aqua

60 soulful contemplative shell pumice pebble

86 dynamic sexy persimmon berry rose

112 relaxed restful lavender blue indigo

138 fresh stimulating turquoise lime leaf

166 designers guild fabric and wallpaper directory   170 designers guild stockists   172 acknowledgments

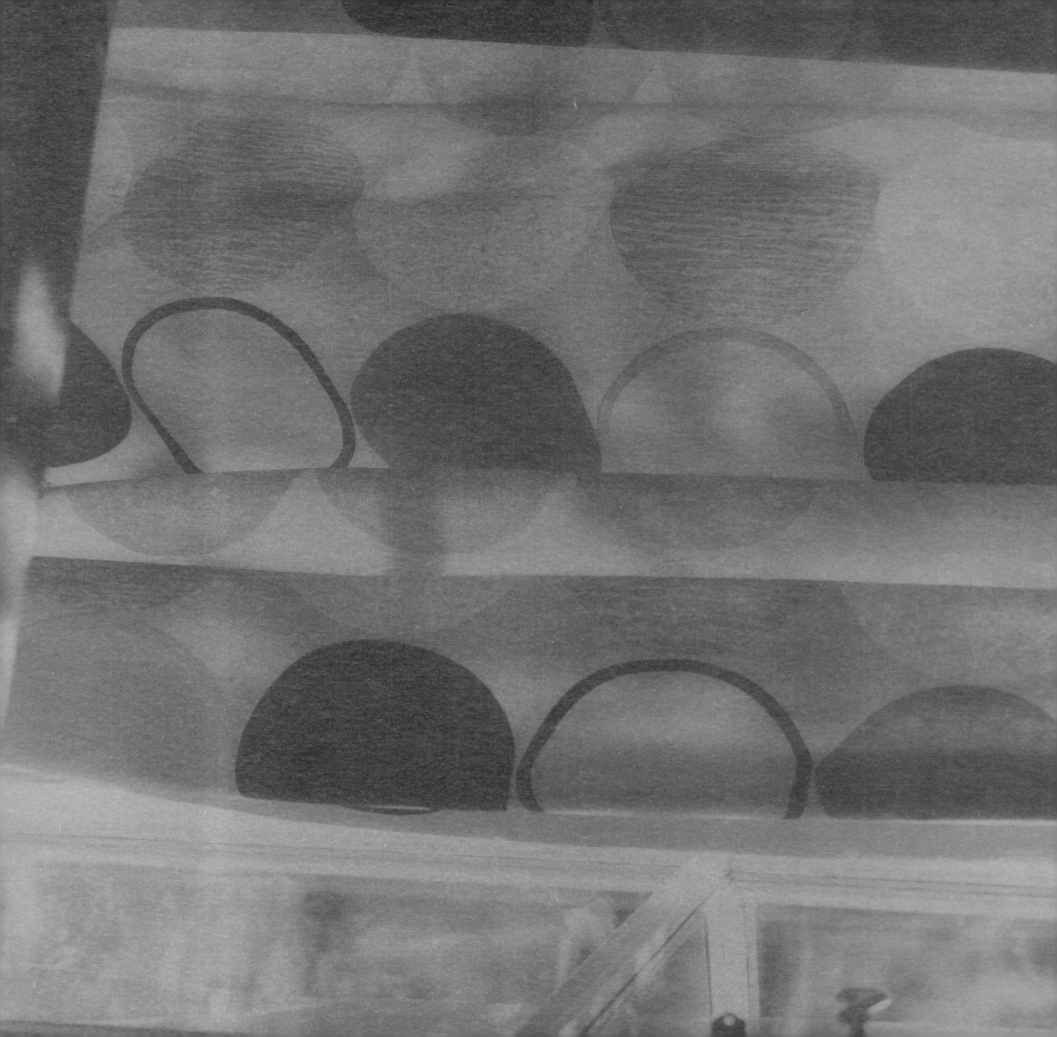

joyful

vivacious

mandarin

citrus

cerise

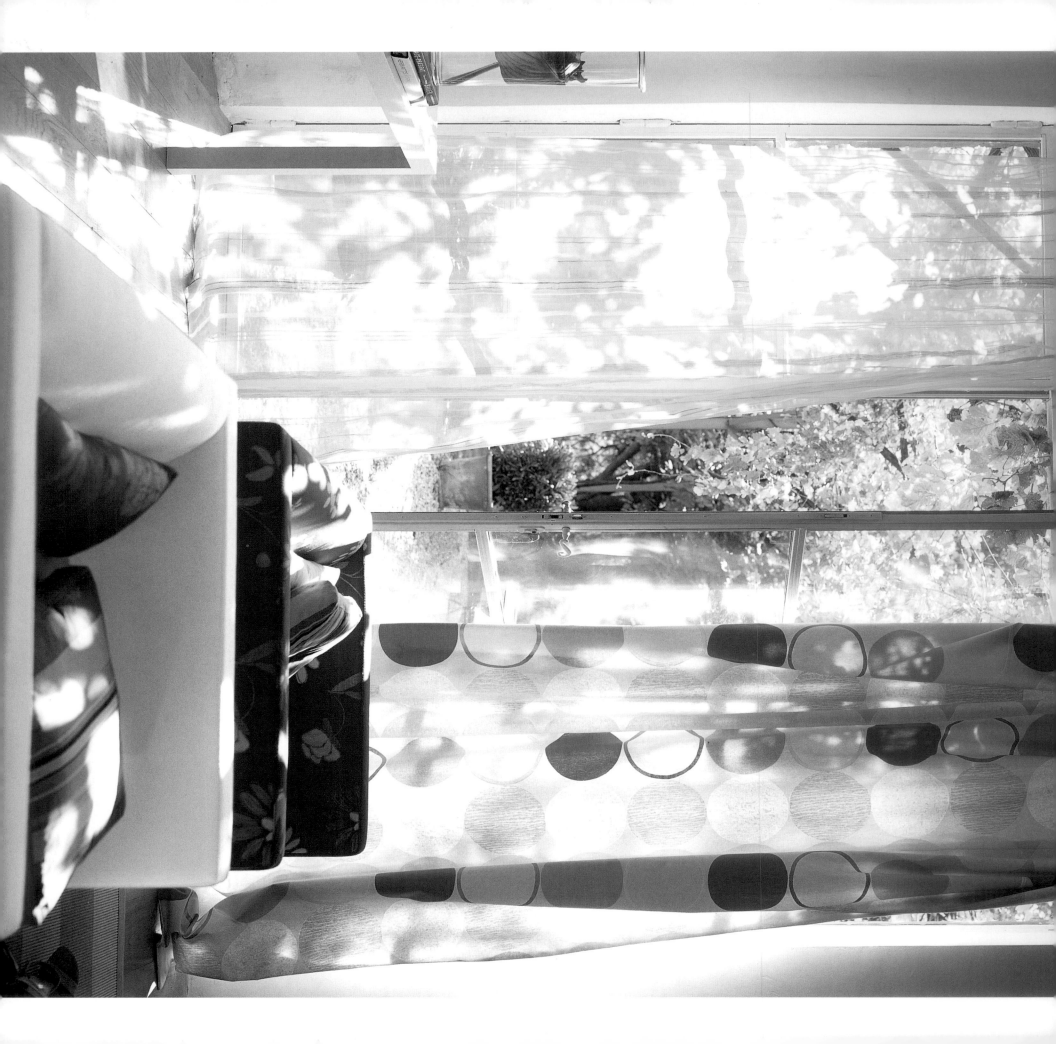

a joyful mix of color and pattern

Often it is the quality of natural light that leads the way when decorating a room. When this French farmhouse was modernized, huge metal-framed windows were inserted to let in the light, and the glorious sunshine that floods the room is one of the keys to its exuberant mood. Filtered first by the leaves outside and then by the bold colors and patterns on the drapes, it paints the entire room in pools of dappled sunlight. The colors were chosen to accentuate this joyful feeling. Fresh citrus shades seem to soak up the light so they can radiate sunshine even on dull days, while the bright lime-greens and yellows bring the wild leafiness of the garden into the orchestrated architecture of the house. The use of translucent voiles and fine-weave cottons at the windows ensures that none of the luminous light is lost. The color contrasts are dynamic and unexpected—the tangy freshness of persimmon contrasting with powder pink, acid green, and touches of turquoise and yellow in the bold floral prints.

Clean lines and contrasting colors have transformed this old house into a fresh, joyful, contemporary space. There is still just a hint of the rustic in the old paneled doors and wooden beams, but the mood is upbeat and modern. The bold geometry of the modern windows contributes immeasurably to the rest of the room.

It's the dynamic mix of color and pattern that gives the room its modern edge; the grid of the square windowpanes is echoed in the lines of the chairs and tables, the circles on the drapes, and the spots and stripes on the pillows. The floral print on the chairs acknowledges the rural location, but forget about chintz, these are boxy clean-cut designs and the flowers are splashy, bold, and modern. Mixed with bold graphic circles and brightly-contrasting stripes, they challenge traditional perceptions of country style. Likewise, the real flowers in this room have a startling modern edge. Instead of big, blowsy bunches there are simple, almost minimalist combinations of flowers and foliage in plain glass vases that lift the mood and complement the clean modern shapes of the furniture. Together with the cutting edge coffee table, chairs and stools, they continue the interesting dynamic between ancient and contemporary, country and modern, that makes this room so striking.

"This wonderfully dynamic mixture of color and pattern—big graphic circles with clashing stripes and splashy modern flower prints—creates a mood of joyful spontaneity that belies the care with which the scheme was put together. The potentially wayward mixture works because of the subtle backdrop of neutrals and whites—the clean oak boards, the neutral-striped rug, the background color of the curtains, the pair of white armchairs and other white furniture." TG

the essence of summer

Continue the mood of joyful exuberance in the way you serve food in a room. Here, a simple summer breakfast of coffee, homemade bread, and jelly is brought alive by the addition of fresh flower heads from the garden and sprigs of mint adorning freshly squeezed orange juice and fruit preserves. The concept of breakfast in bed is comforting, but here the presentation is unquestionably modern, with flower heads floated in water and the selection of different preserves spooned into clear glass pots. A pretty white tablecloth and napkins embroidered with flowers pulls it all together and allows the bright colors to sing out in the sunshine.

"When using flowers to decorate food choose their colors to complement each other and it will look as mouthwatering as it tastes. People can be reticent about using just the heads of long-stemmed flowers, but there are times when that is how they look most beautiful. You don't necessarily need vases—these dahlias are gorgeous just floating on water in a simple ceramic bowl. Sprigs of fresh mint add a welcome note of green and impart their refreshing smell and flavor, making it a feast for all the senses."TG

glamorous color, sensual texture

strong shapes and soft textures give this living space a joyful, flirtatious air

The key to this room is the daring combination of color and texture. Velvet is an old-fashioned fabric, but here—thanks to the bright, vivacious colors and the clean graphic shapes of the furniture—it looks uncompromisingly modern. The hibiscus orange, shocking pink, and clear turquoise-blue can all be found in the colors of the drapes—an up-to-date paisley design. What makes them work so well together is that all three have equal intensity—one is not stronger than another, enabling them to contrast rather than conflict. The shiny, white curves of the molded chairs, lamp, and ceramics add an extra exciting note of contrasting texture against the warm, worn terra-cotta floor.

a feeling of space and light

This wonderful, high-ceilinged apartment is in a converted schoolhouse—a clean, modern, urban space with great proportions. The size of the rooms perfectly complements the tall arched windows and there is a welcome feeling of space and light above the hubbub of the city.

It can be hard to know how to arrange your life in such a large open-plan layout. Keep things simple—too many elements look cluttered and fussy while large, clean shapes and clear colors build the structure you need. Here, even the textures have been confined to just two—hard and soft. All the fabric furnishings are in linen—a soft yet flat texture that does not detract from the essentially square and masculine lines of the furniture. The only other textures are the hard glass, metal, and shiny white surfaces of the modern tables, lamps, and sideboard.

The use of color is what creates the mood, manipulating the space, creating different atmospheres in different areas for different uses, but drawing them subtly together. Instead of keeping the place all white—the classic response to a large open-plan loft—a restricted palette of just a few strong tonal shades gives these two large adjoining rooms a sparkling vitality often lacking in such spaces.

In the upper room (right and overleaf), the orange on the sofa is a subtle shade of cantaloupe—one tone down from the zingy citrus notes seen earlier. This sits beautifully beside the fresh chartreuse of the armchair, the pale ocean on the footstool, and the clear crocus-mauve at the windows. Just one mauve pillow on the sofa makes the crucial link with the crocus fabric at the windows.

The space flows down past the staircase into another living room on a lower level, with slightly smaller proportions. Here, slightly cooler colors lower the mood a note or two. But while the temperature may be cooler, the vital, vivacious mood is sustained. The ocean colors link both spaces, but the cantaloupe-orange of the sofa has been exchanged for lime, with accents of turquoise in small details, such as the pillows on the sofa and floor. Small touches such as these help give each room an identity of its own, even if some of the principal colors have been carried over into both.

vital, uplifting color against a white backdrop

These are vital rather than vivid colors, with a clarity and purity that instantly lifts the spirits. A deliberately low-key backdrop of white walls and a polished resin floor lets the colors ring out in the open, uncluttered space, while other details such as pillows, lamps, tables, and other furniture are also confined to white.

Heavy, opulent drapes can look out of place in minimalist modern spaces, so here, banners of plain fabric have been suspended on metal poles to make simple shades that can be opened or shut, depending on the quality of light and privacy required. They also take the color in the room right up to the ceiling. The same window treatment has been used throughout the apartment, but in the lower room just one window panel is colored; the rest remain pure white, which creates a cooler feeling around the windows. Again, white is the predominant color in the backdrop of walls and floor, with fresh white linen pillows and a leather chair and stool.

a crisp striped cloth and a scattering of petals for a spontaneous alfresco lunch

shaded olive trees, summer lunch

This table laid for lunch outside has a casual, carefree charm—a mismatch of chairs brought out into the garden in the shade of old olive and fig trees. What makes it so inviting, however, is the clever use of color, which belies the apparently spontaneous arrangement. The orange of the Arne Jacobsen chairs is highlighted in the wonderfully vibrant striped cloth, and echoed in the flower heads strewn around the place settings and tucked into tiny vases with a few scented geranium leaves.

"Eating outside is liberating—the simple act of setting a table outdoors frees us from the formalities that might prevail in the house. Take a few risks—mix old and new, rustic and contemporary—but keep it all lively with a subtle continuity of color. Choosing furniture and cloths to use can be a lot of fun. Pick a favorite piece of fabric and work around it, or take some chairs that work well together and continue the scheme around those colors. Fresh salad leaves, herbs, and nasturtiums from the garden, make a colorful delicious salad." TC

a feast for all the senses

Use flowers and leaves creatively to add to the spontaneous spirit of an alfresco lunch. Don't reach automatically for a pitcher or vase—gather flower heads from the garden or from arrangements inside the house. When flowers in a vase begin to fade, there are always a few blooms whose beauty remains intact. Pick off the flower heads that still have life in them, and scatter them over a tablecloth or display them singly in little glass vases where they can be admired close-up. This is a great way to make the most of your flowers, even if they only last like this for a short time. They can even be kept in the refrigerator for a few days in advance, if required. The heads of guernsey lilies or single gladiolus blooms, usually seen at the top of long stately stems and in the company of other flowers, are transformed when used in this simple, unassuming way. They add to that sense of "contemplated haphazardness" which is so appealing but can be quite hard to achieve. Edible flowers, such as nasturtiums and pansies and freshly picked herbs such as chervil, cilantro, and basil, can be used to decorate and add taste to salads. When serving cool drinks, such as fresh lemonade, fill the glass with slices of lemon or lime and use sprigs of mint to flavor the drink and make it more refreshing.

dancing rhythms and vibrant stripes

"The striped fabric is what draws this whole scheme together. It's perfect for this room, as it relates to the severe geometry of the floor and at the same time contains almost all the other colors that are used elsewhere. Using a plain fabric for the seats of the sofa defines its shape and gives a neutral base for the other patterns." TG

Sometimes it is worth being as bold as you dare to breathe new life into a space. This historic room, with its old wood-paneled doors and black-and-white tiled floor, could easily look heavy and old-fashioned. Instead, it has been taken to the opposite extreme with a quirky, modern mix of bright color and graphic pattern. A real sense of joy has been brought into the space, with vivid stripes, exuberant florals, and cheerful clashes of bright orange, mauve, pink, and canary yellow.

But there is method in the madness: the scheme is held together by a few subtle color continuities which save it from fragmenting. The geometric floor is one anchoring force; the charcoal color is repeated in the striped fabric on the sofas and in the floral fabrics and rug, with their scribbly, graphic, almost 1950s feel. The use of bright yellow, leapfrogging from the drapes to the floral pillows on the sofa and ottoman, is another. This is a bold look, which works because of the severity of the floor and the subtle repeating relationships between the colors, like recurring jazz themes. The flowers—tall stems of alliums or guernsey lilies, or papery rounds of ranunculus layered in stripes of color under water—continue the quirky, graphic style.

accents of orange and cerise pink

When accents of pink and orange are used in a mainly white room, the mood is warm, fresh, and joyful. The grand architecture of this French chateau, with its ornate paneling, soaring ceilings, and high shuttered windows, has been given a young, contemporary feel with low furniture and vivacious, feminine color. Comfortable modern sofas and chairs are joined by lots of floor pillows—sitting on the floor in a room like this immediately makes it feel informal and relaxed. The windows are dressed in layers and stripes of various shades of pink, with gauzy voile filtering the light like colored glass. The pattern is a modern take on printed lace—just right for this charming flirtatious mood.

"The use of color here is gloriously tonal—taking pink from palest shell to shocking Schiaparelli, with accents of persimmon and mauve. Color contrast is provided by the vast expanses of white paneled walls, and the oversized white rug, which lightens the effect of the wooden floor. Modern combinations of hot pink dahlias, spiky grasses, and scented green geranium leaves give a freshness and vitality to the room." TG

pure

serene

mauve

sea green

aqua

a new tranquillity

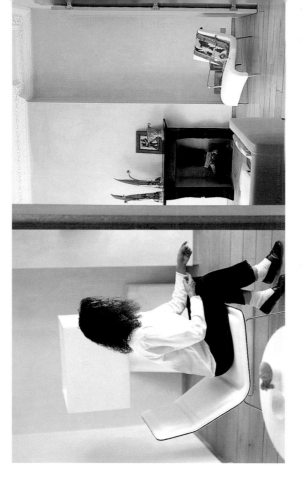

Sometimes just one major alteration—such as repainting a wall or reupholstering a sofa—can lead the way for a number of smaller, more subtle changes that combine to change the overall feeling of a room.

This large double living space now has a serene and tranquil air, thanks to a subtle change of color. Walls that were once a deep turquoise have been replastered in pale *eau de nil*, which is complemented by the existing clear aqua paintwork. Bare floorboards allow the eye to run unimpeded from one end of the room to another, while translucent drapes contribute to the almost ethereal mood. The room not only looks but feels different.

Lots of pure white further lifts the space—a comfortable large sofa and modern chair are upholstered in crisp white linen, while the contemporary shapes of a white leather chair, a large Capellini floor lamp, and low tables in molded plastic and metal provide some contrasting textures. There is an interesting play between hard and soft, shiny and matte, plain and pattern, which keeps the room alive.

In such a calm and soothing space, the few splashes of contrasting color and pattern stand out to great effect—the bold floral fabric on the floor pillow and back of a chair has as much impact as the painting on the mantel. Color and pattern have also been used to draw the two ends of the room together and make them work as one space—this can be surprisingly difficult to achieve in double or 'knock-through' living areas. Keeping the main upholstery colors of white and mauve the same at either end, and sprinkling accents of aqua, ocean, and green in the form of pillows and other details throughout, is an extremely effective way of unifying the space. Note the way the two strongest patterns—the jazzy stripe and the cut-velvet peony print—have been repeated just once in both spaces; you don't need to overdo it. The stripe on the pillows is so bold that the eye is drawn to it even from the far end of the room. The beautiful mauve and white orchid blooms are a decorative force on their own, anchoring the eye in the center of the room and playing on the other mauve accents.

"This is the third change the living room has undergone since we've lived in this house. I wanted a softer mood while still wishing to experiment with color—the paler walls and a lot more white have created an entirely new mood. This is a light, airy look for the warmer months, but in winter I might use more color by laying down rugs and changing the pillows. It interests me to see how these subtle changes can mold the whole feeling and emotional charge of a room." TG

Furnishings have been kept deliberately simple in this light, uncluttered space. The absence of a rug on the floor not only makes the room feel larger, it also plays off the contrasting modern shapes and textures against a neutral, organic backdrop of pale oak boards. The mood is clear and linked by a subtle continuity of color between the two ends of the room and by soft recurring shapes and textures. The resulting harmonies are as seductive to the eye as soft music is to the ear.

modern flowers for a summer party

The same room has been transformed for a party with the addition of stunning modern flowers, presenting old favorites-in new ways that break all the rules. A posy of sweet peas, roses, and peonies is combined with towering calla lilies and a single pink guernsey lily in a curved vase, while peonies and hydrangea heads are submerged in water, their saturated colors glowing through the glass. There are startling uses of more flowers such as Allium schubertii, its glorious mauve sprays exploding from green glass like a great flowery firework. Unexpected colors, shapes, and textures delight the eye at every turn—the delicacy of tiny roses and sweet peas offset by spearlike leaves and spindly seed heads.

a new mood of calm

This dining room was formerly much more rustic in style and had a completely different atmosphere—a few simple changes have altered the mood entirely. Although, the color of the wall remains the same textured lime-green, this time a tiny modern painting now hangs on the wall, looking wonderfully out of scale on a huge, bare expanse, and much more modern furniture has been used. Minimal glass-fronted metal cupboards house ceramics and glasses, while a large square table in soft gray powder-coated metal is an imposing presence in this low open space.

This room is at ground level, and has lower ceilings than the rest of the house. It could easily have ended up feeling quite dark, but the wide expanse of windows opening onto the garden, the pale stone floor, and the simple low shapes of the furniture keep the space light and uncluttered. Against the pared-down minimalism of the table and cupboards and almost-bare wall, the snaky S-shapes of Tom Dixon's raffia chairs have a gloriously organic, almost sculptural impact and provide an interesting change of texture. In one corner of the room, where a sofa and chairs are grouped around a cozy open fire, plaid fabrics and textured embroidery have been replaced by simple white linen upholstery and pillows in clear tonal shades.

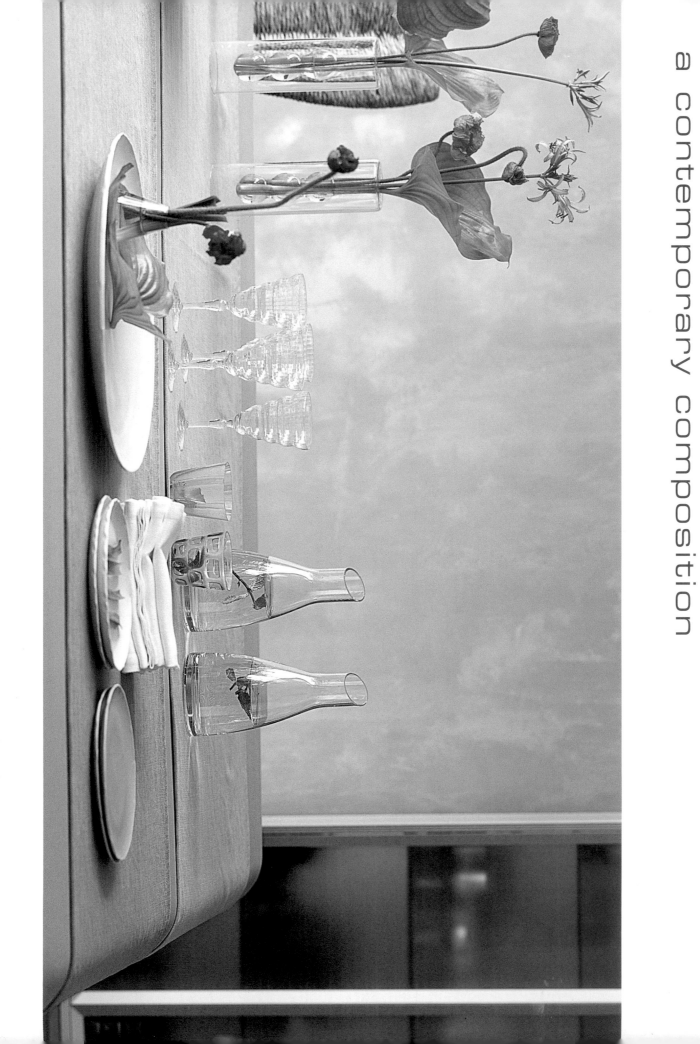

a contemporary composition

However pleasing a calming, low-key space can be, you may wish to make it more lively and celebratory for a party. Be simple at the same time as being creative and add elegance and a sense of occasion to the room without destroying its peaceful mood. Compose the table as an artist might do an abstract painting: your paints are the cloths, napkins, glasses, and ceramics, and, of course, the food itself.

"Create a table setting that is stimulating and adds to the air of enjoyment and anticipation. Here, four chilled soups have been elegantly arranged in lines on strips of pale linen—each with a different fresh herb leaf. The wonderful rich colors of the soups are reflected in the poppy flowers. Allow the shapes and colors of the food to set the style." IG

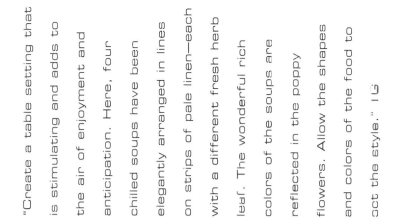

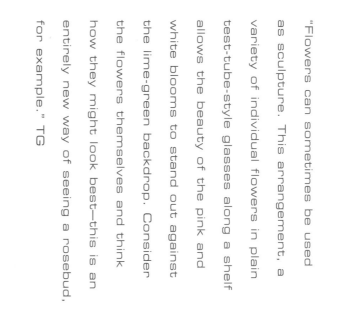

"Flowers can sometimes be used as sculpture. This arrangement, a variety of individual flowers in plain test-tube-style glasses along a shelf allows the beauty of the pink and white blooms to stand out against the lime-green backdrop. Consider the flowers themselves and think how they might look best—this is an entirely new way of seeing a rosebud, for example." TG

a scattering of pink rose petals for a summer celebration

softens the geometry of a city garden

summer garden party

This garden has a strong graphic design, with its white stone steps, clipped topiary cubes, and inner sanctum within a square of bleached lime trees. With the addition of simple cube stools in soft pink, fuchsia, and white, some grouped on a zinc square in the center, the view from an upstairs window resembles an abstract painting. For the party, hundreds of pink and red rose petals have been heaped on tables and scattered on the surface of the pond—a simple yet romantic and somehow exotic touch—pervading the air with their heady scent. Soft pillows for relaxing on the terrace are shaded by panels of pink-and-white fabric.

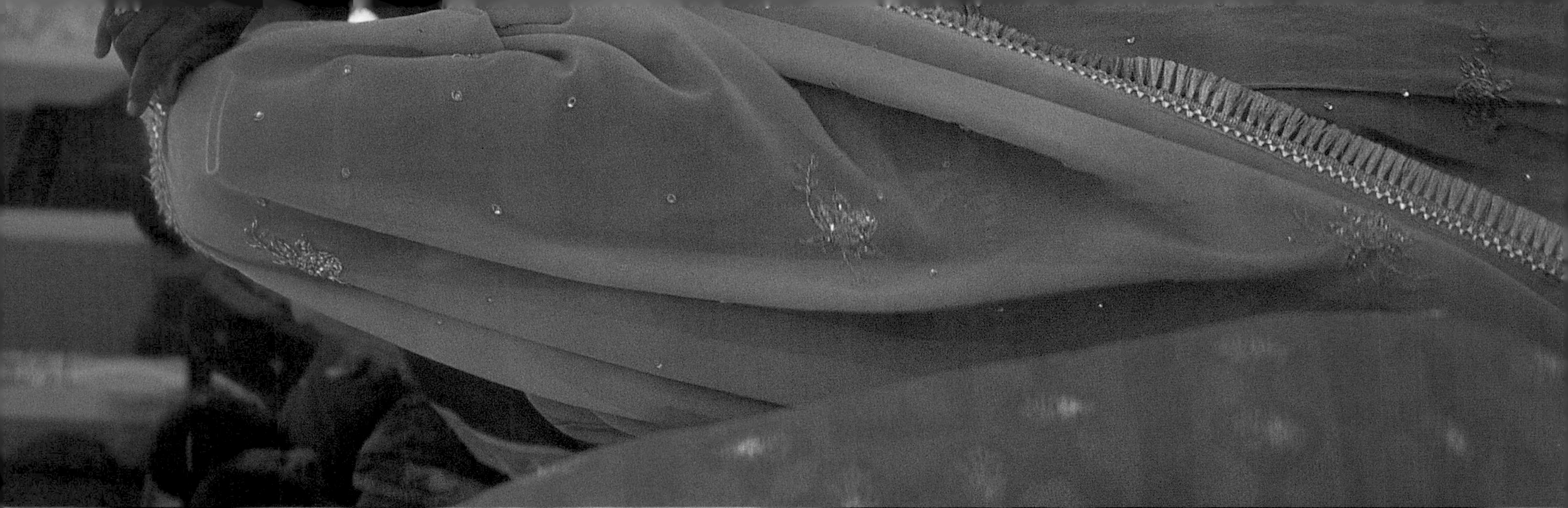

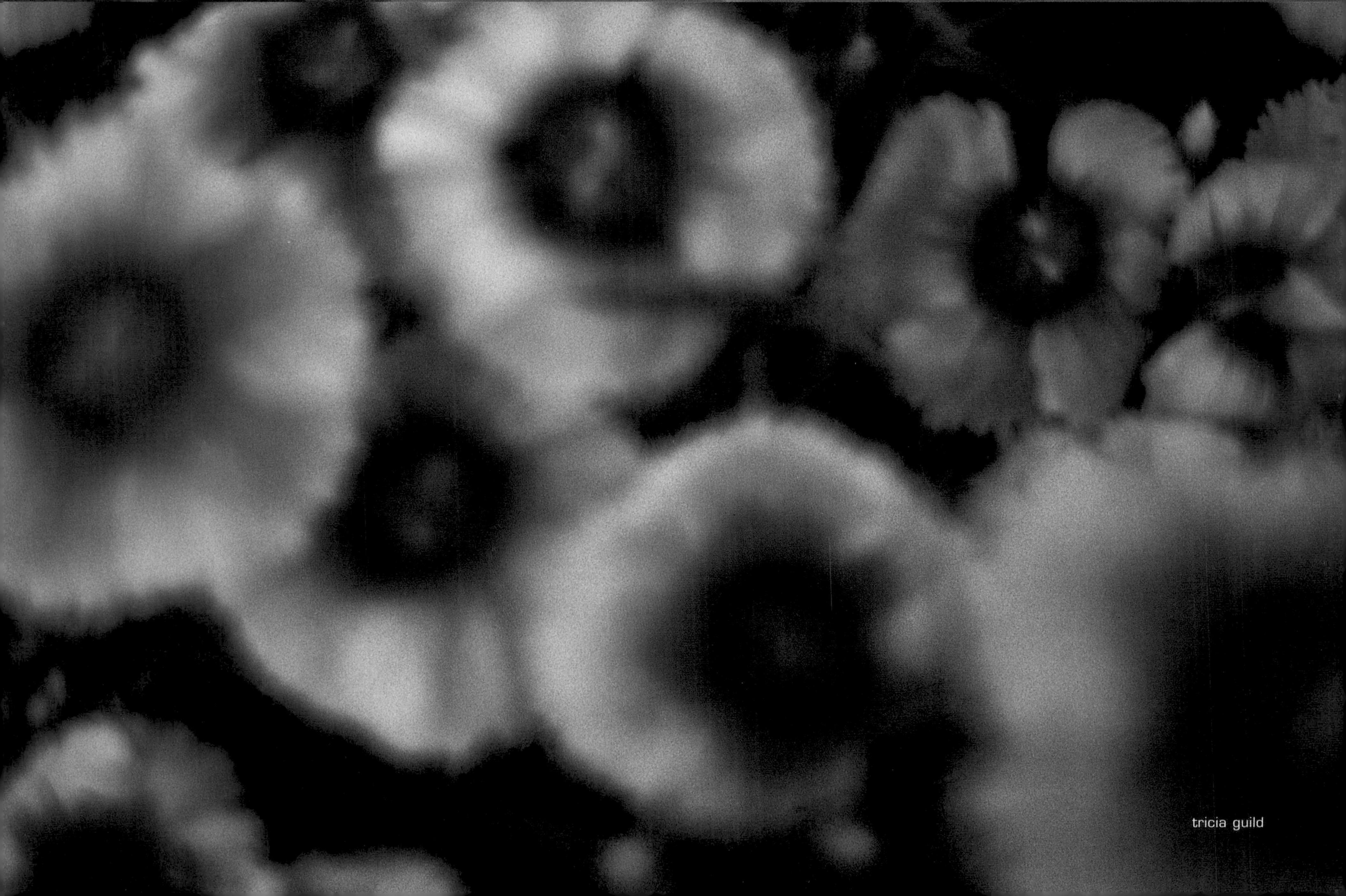

tricia guild

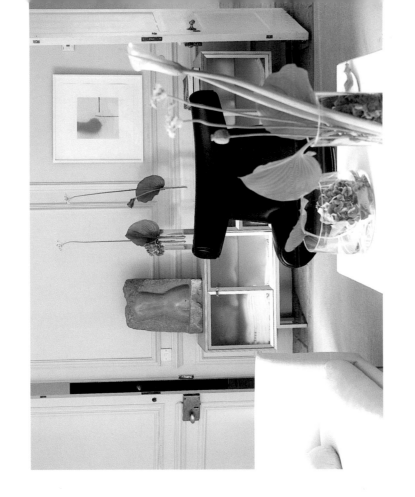

Contemporary furniture does not need to be confined to large minimalist lofts, and period features don't have to cramp your style. Mixing old and new in an interior is not only fashionable and exciting, it's a great way to breathe life into an older house, accentuating its timeless beauty in a bold and unexpected way.

This English manor has strong traditional architecture that could easily have dictated a dark and old-fashioned style of decorating. Instead, a well-judged use of cool, clear color and contemporary furniture has carved out a modern and soothing space, perfectly in tune with the soft morning light that streams through the mullioned windows. The original wood-paneled walls have been washed with a beautiful, soft, sea-green paint, which immediately makes the space feel light and up-to-date without clashing with its period details and flagstone floor. Much of the floor has been covered with a rug in palest duck-egg blue so that the furniture sits on a clean contemporary "island," with just a strip of the beautifully textured old floor visible as a contrast around the edges.

The cool colors determined the choice of furniture—tables and chairs that are comfortable but uncompromisingly modern in shape, shade, and texture. The black leather armchair, a contemporary classic with a masculine, tailored feel, is quite unexpected—the softness of the leather contrasting with the shiny metal legs. It looks absolutely right, and inhabits the room almost like a piece of sculpture. The other pieces of furniture—a wonderfully comfortable club chair in ink-green bouclé wool and a large, low sofa in pale ocean linen—retreat happily into the background.

There is a lot of white—on the ceiling, in the floor lamp, on the coffee-table, and in the voluminous linen drapes. The tall white calla lilies and alliums, fanning out into the space, perfectly suit the restrained elegance of this room—even the green of their stems and calyxes picks up on some of the other colors. To bring in accents of brighter color, the drapes are edged with a bright sea-green silk cuff, and there are pillows in lime and chartreuse. These help give the room its sense of perfect balance—without them it might have felt almost too cool.

"The unexpectedness of this curvaceous, dramatic chair in the cool, calm restraint of its surroundings gives this room necessary tension. The black, tailored leather brings a masculine, almost dangerous edge to the space. It doesn't appear overbearing because subtle touches of black and charcoal in the etchings and other details help to anchor it in the room." TG

elegance in the detail

The old-and-new theme has been carried through to the details of how food and drink are served, both inside and in the garden which leads off this room. Ice cream, homemade cookies, and liqueurs are presented in a style as pure and elegant as the room itself. Mismatching antique glasses are partnered with handmade modern plates in a clear blue that picks up the darker mauve-blue of the hydrangea heads. The touches of green in the leaves used in the flower arrangements and presentation of the food add an extra "lift" to the overall scheme of the room, bringing some of the freshness of the garden inside and the style of the interior to the garden.

"Hydrangeas are a popular garden flower that has fallen out of fashion, but if you really look at them they are so beautiful and their colors so subtle. Cutting off the giant flower heads and arranging them in simple glass vases or under water helps you to appreciate them in a new light. It interests me to use leaves and flowers in unusual ways—these leaves, for example, add a graphic touch to the plate of cookies." TG

a peaceful mood

Soft pale green is an ideal color for a bedroom—cool and calming without being cold. Here, the walls are a slightly chalky green, and there are accents of ocean, lime, and *eau de nil*. This room has quite a dark wooden floor, but placing the bed on its own natural-colored rug helps to lighten up the room, as do the translucent drapes in broad stripes of subtly different patterns. Pure, crisp, white linen is welcoming on a bed, and the more formal flower pattern on the throw—blue hydrangeas with hand-painted leaves—is a reminder that, for all its fresh, modern furnishings, this is an old country house.

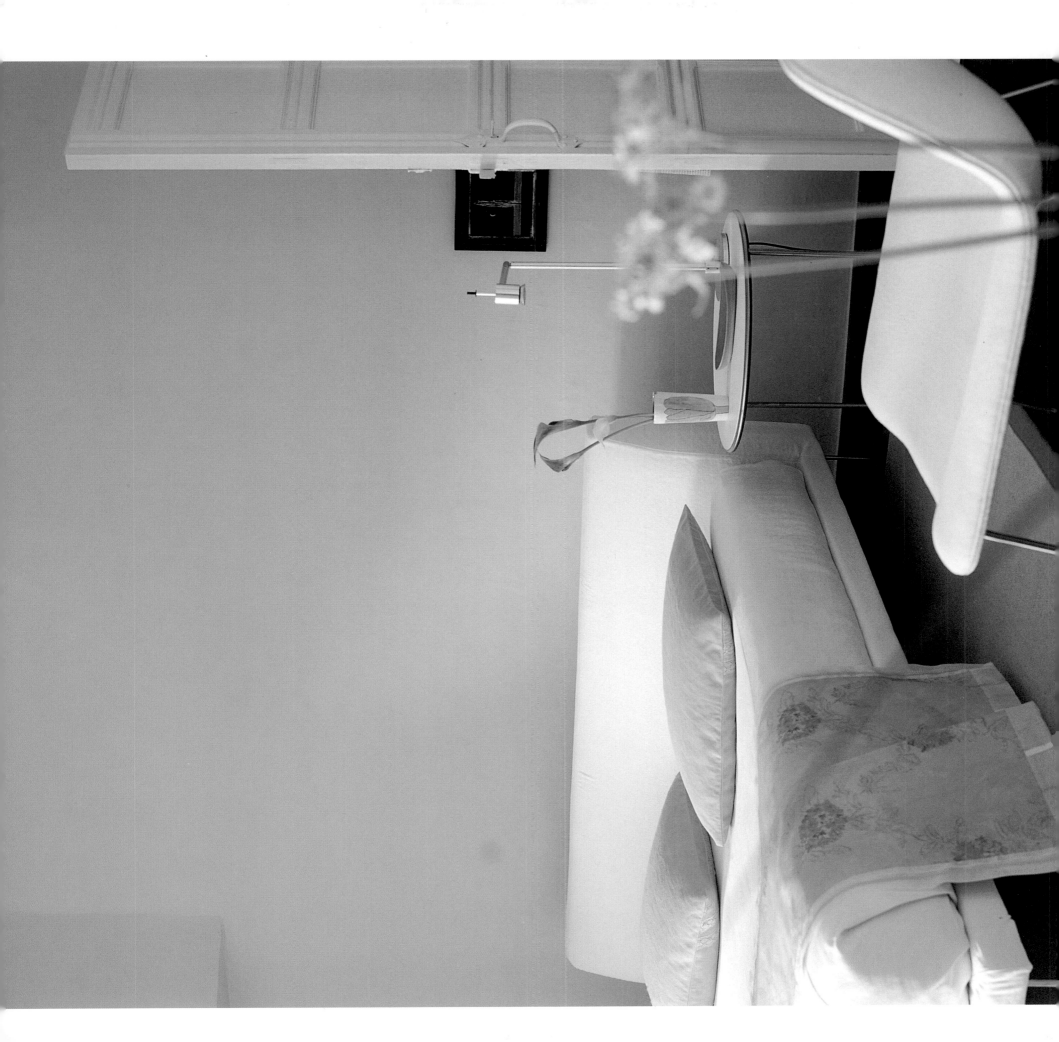

soulful

contemplative

shell

pumice

pebble

a space to dream

"Light, feminine fabrics on the bed and at the window bring a dreamy quality to this otherwise quite cool contemporary bedroom and form a bridge between the old architectural details and the modern furniture. Just a single piece of crumpled lightweight muslin softens the clean metal frame of the four-poster, making it romantic but still resolutely modern. The drape is a banner of the same muslin that will float anywhere along the pole." TG

The restful feeling in this room is a result of its combination of natural colors and textures: the stone and old beams of the architecture, the warm wooden floor, the cool metal frames of the furniture, and the crisp linen on the beds. Just one shade—a pale pink so soft it is almost a neutral—has been added to inject a degree of freshness and warmth. But this is not a frilly, feminine pink. The clean lines of the contemporary bed and daybed are upholstered and made up with a minimum of fuss. Lots of plain linen, simple square pillows, and a few panels of subtly patterned and embroidered fabric are used. This is a perfect space for sleeping, reading, or relaxing.

Most of the room's interest lies in the surprise of finding modern furniture alongside such old architecture. The pieces have a clean-lined elegance and an unexpected lightness. The daybed on its metal frame seems almost to float above the floor, while the bed is a spare four-poster in pale brushed-steel, draped with a single white muslin panel. Against the backdrop of the mullioned windows, the modern oval table and white leather chairs set up an interesting contrast in period and style.

It is easier to create a soulful mood in high-ceilinged spaces; here, to draw the eye upward, the curtain pole has been fixed as close to the ceiling as possible and hung with banners of fabric that stretch right down to the floor. This increases the feeling of height in the room and makes the windows appear larger. White muslin with a thin pink stripe filters the sun and floods the room with soft, hazy light; the panel of fabric can be pulled into different positions along the rail as needed. The slim uprights of the modern four-poster and the tall slice of mirror propped up against the wall emphasize the strong vertical element of the room. The minimalist arrangements of white alliums, pink guernsey lilies, and single orchid and gladiolus blooms are the perfect complement to the still and tranquil mood. Beautiful and graceful without being fussy, the bright pink color highlights the more subtle use of pink elsewhere.

The details in a neutral room make all the difference, and they can be easily changed to create a new feel. Here, the only accessories are tonal, in deeper or richer shades of pink or subtle stripes and patterns.

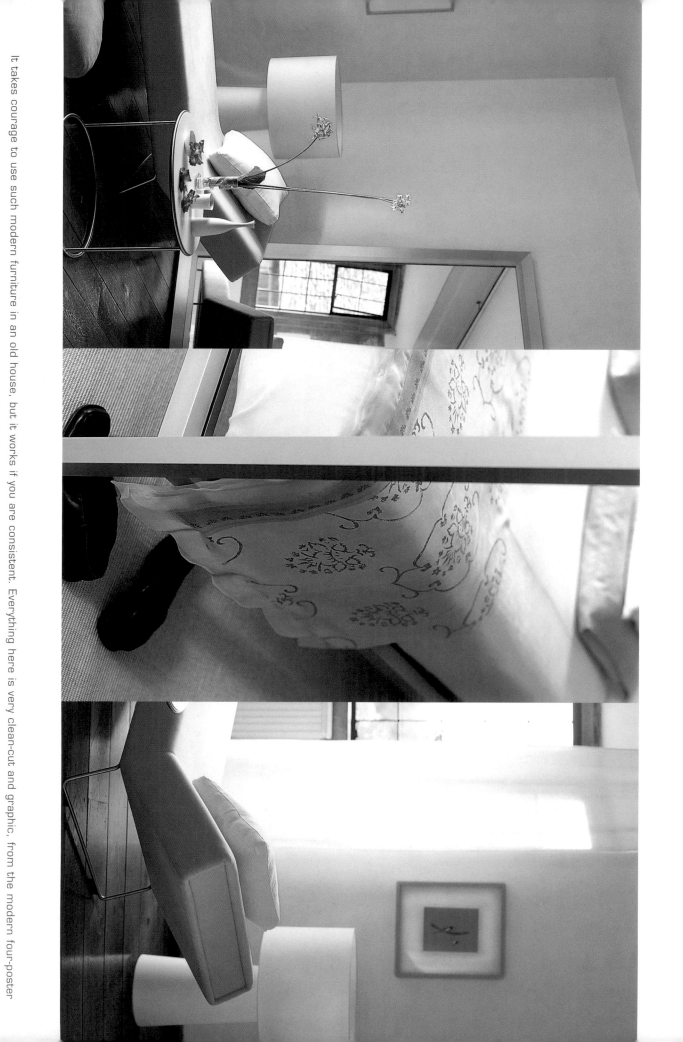

shell pink so pale and soft it's barely there

It takes courage to use such modern furniture in an old house, but it works if you are consistent. Everything here is very clean-cut and graphic, from the modern four-poster to the light metal frames of the daybed and tables. There is a balance of square geometrics and curvaceous rounded shapes—they play off each other in a satisfying way. The soft, dreamy touches are in the details—in the scattering of pink gladiolus blooms on the table and the delicately patterned bedspread. There is so little pattern elsewhere in this room that even the tiniest details, like the hand-painted scrolling designs on the fabric, are noticeable.

"Old and new contrast harmoniously in the circular white table and white leather chairs by the old mullioned windows. There's even a quiet thoughtfulness in the way the table has been set for breakfast. It might take a little extra effort to bring everything up to the bedroom and arrange the fruit and yogurt in little glasses with sprigs of mint, but the reward is a beautiful, stylish start to the day." TC

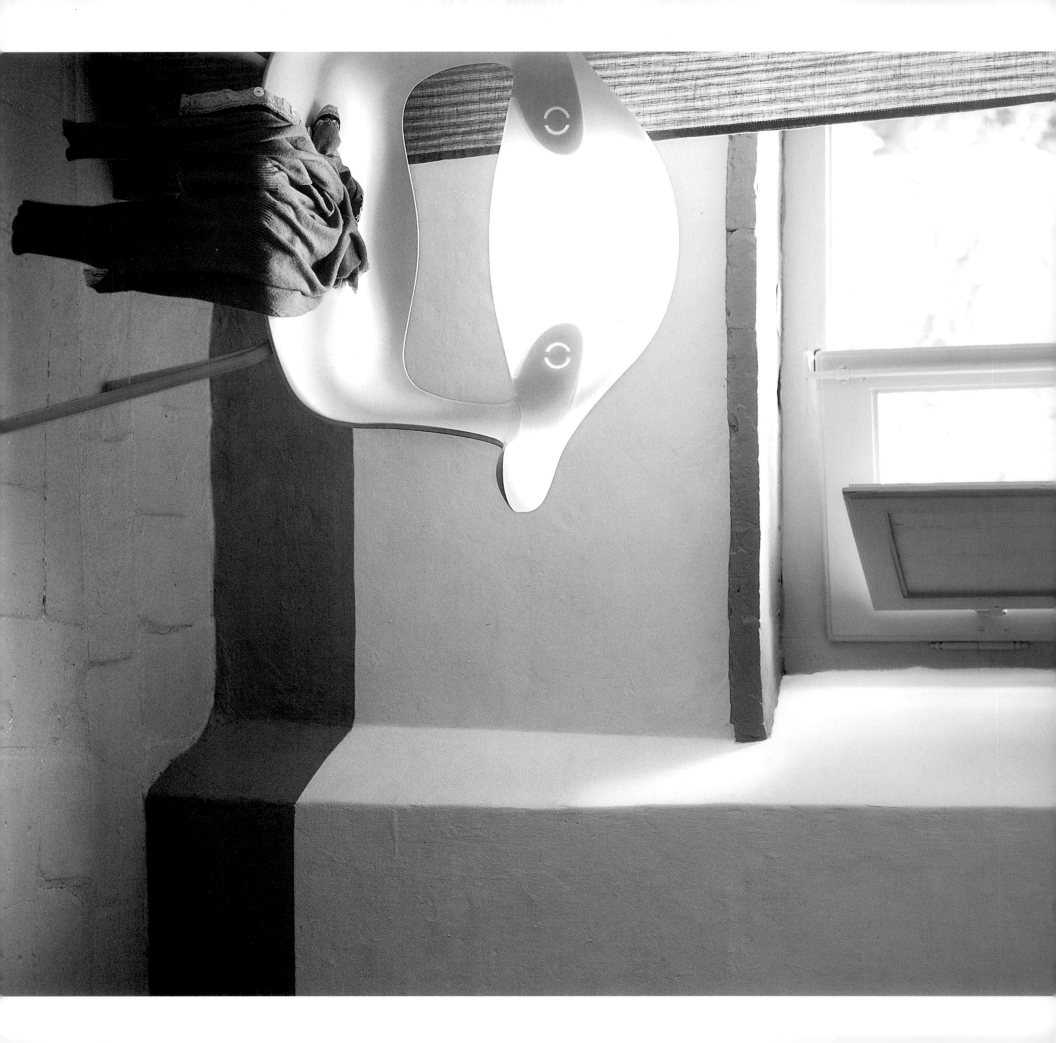

cool composition

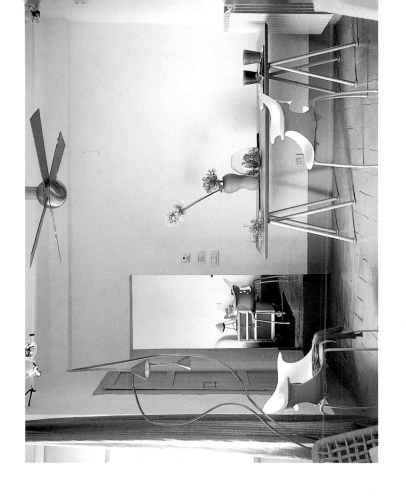

There is a masculine but tranquil atmosphere in this tiny apartment in an old palazzo in Tuscany. With an abundance of distinctive architectural features, the aim was to make the studio feel clean, uncluttered, and modern. Paring down the color and keeping the furniture simple was the key to success, and the tiled floor was painted gray throughout to unify the space. The modern steel kitchen is a miniature model of efficiency, while brushed aluminum tables and cabinets look light and elegant in a soft gray. This is far from soulless minimalism, however. Touches such as a propeller-style ceiling fan and metal lamps give the place an air of individuality and character. It is the perfect male pied-à-terre—a peaceful haven when solitude is desired, but with the potential to become a practical, sociable base for entertaining.

Gray is the predominant color, with matte and shiny metal sitting easily alongside the various tonal shades. An absence of stronger colors makes the variations in shades and textures and the different moods that the various materials evoke more apparent. One principal piece of furniture—a wedge of a modern sofa in pale blue-gray linen—presides over the main space; other seating consists of informal floor pillows and woven rope chairs on light metal frames. The transparent quality of this natural rope weave adds a new texture and makes the space feel open and uncluttered.

In all this modernity, the magic of a real fire has not been forgotten, and a contemporary fireplace has been cut into a long, low opening in the wall. The result is unquestionably modern, but still preserves the tradition of glowing embers and wood smoke, so welcome in the cold Tuscan winters. The low furniture is grouped informally around a rug with a geometric design in the same tonal colors, creating a quiet yet intimate mood. Metal lamps inject a slightly humorous note, and their light unobtrusive structure is the perfect complement to the rope chairs and table.

Essentially this is an exercise in the use of noncolor, but touches of mauve raise the prevailing grays onto a richer, more soulful plane. Flowers, a matte vase, and the odd pillow keep the mauve theme moving through the various different rooms—the space would feel much colder and overly masculine without them.

"Painting the floor tiles a soft gray has helped to lighten and unify the space. A slightly richer gray border has been painted around the base of the walls—a modern take on a traditional Italian decorating device which gives weight to the room and balances the fine tubular furniture. Gray paint has also been used for windows and doors giving shape, and a reminder that we are within an ancient building." TG

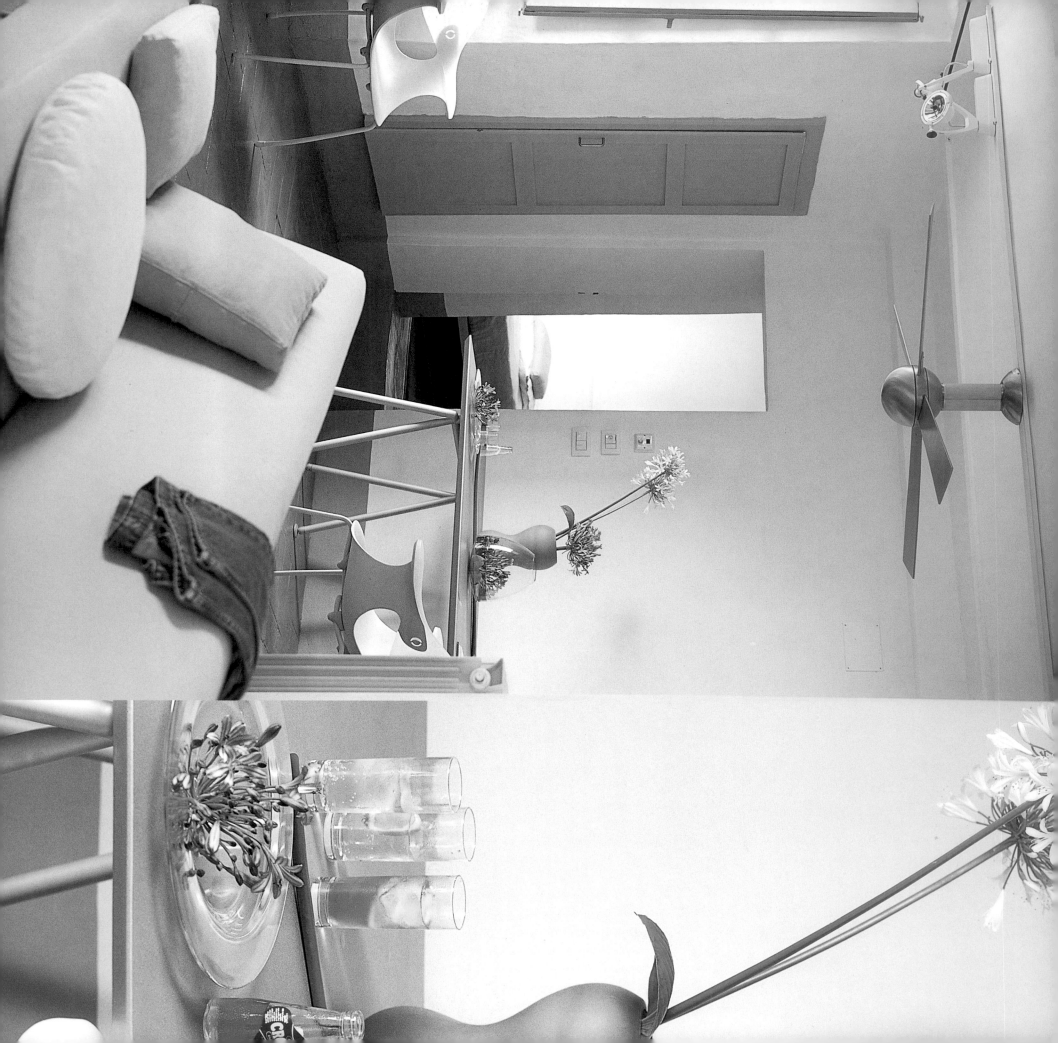

In such a small apartment, the same mood, colors, and details carried throughout all the rooms create a restful harmony and make the space feel larger. The tiny bedroom is just big enough for a double bed on a brushed-steel frame, some metal storage units, and a white molded plastic chair for clothes, while the contemporary-style kitchen continues the theme with angular stainless steel units echoing the gray-on-gray scheme of the rest of the apartment.

splashes of impromptu color bring a blank canvas to life

"In this neutral environment even the most casual, throwaway gestures have a startling graphic impact, and any other color added to the mix, even temporarily, really sings out. Slices of orange in a drink, a spotted red tie slung across a chair, or a bowl of bright lemons on a table are like splashes of bright paint on a white-and-gray canvas." TC

soft, silvery shadows

In this city apartment, different shades of grays have been used in the living room while oatmeal tones bring a subtly different look to the bedroom (overleaf). Both looks are contemporary and slightly masculine in feel, while sacrificing nothing to comfort. You could imagine reading for hours undisturbed in this peaceful room.

The temptation with natural schemes is to create textural contrasts, but here that technique has been kept to a minimum, resulting in an almost palpable sense of stillness. In the living room, the predominant textures are quite dry: thick gray latex painted on one wall; a coarse, cotton duck for the gray striped drapes and dove-colored flannel on the sofa. The metal in the room has a soft sheen rather than a shine—the brushed aluminum of the minimalist cupboard, the gleam of a lamp, and the finish on the salvaged and stripped-down radiator. Even the floor—old boards painted white and worn down with wear—has a flatness that is appropriate. Flowers and other objects are kept to a minimum—white Amazon lilies in clear glass vases and a few specially chosen ceramics.

Grays work well together. For deeper accents, choose charcoals rather than the browner shades and taupes that may sit uneasily in the scheme. Mixing gray neutrals with browns and creams is often extremely tricky. In this scheme, the oatmeal shades have been confined to the bedroom (overleaf), thus creating a completely different look while remaining within the overall neutral palette.

One wall in the bedroom has been covered in a subtle flower print—a Japanese-style design that is echoed on the bedlinen. Pattern is unexpected in a minimal scheme, particularly one with such a masculine feel, but this design is about as pared-down as floral gets and contributes to the mood of calm. Again, textures are surprisingly dry. The curtains here are no-nonsense flannel, an unusual choice in a bedroom but with a layer of light voile underneath that plays against it and injects a touch of softness. The bedcover is also flannel, in a deeper chocolate shade, but with piles of soft pillows, one in richly-patterned silk. The shapes in these rooms are gloriously spare—the wide, low bed with its pale wood headboard, the minimalist metal tables and lamps—but the overall feel is one of comfort.

"Neutral tones can be desensitizing, so add some life in the depth of tone. Here, I've included charcoal among the cooler, paler grays in the living room and cocoa brown amid the oatmeal shades of the bedroom. The textures are cool and dry, but a few softening touches make all the difference—the velvet nap of a pillow, the fragility of white flower petals, the gossamer voile of the under-curtains mellow the scheme without compromising its masculinity." TG

Without the subtle flower design on the wall behind the bed, this minimalist bedroom might have looked hard and soulless. A few touches like this one soften the room just enough. The contemporary bed has piles of squashy pillows, most of them plain but one in a delicately patterned silk, and the flannel curtains have a layer of translucent voile underneath. Even the sheen of the curved metal chair beside the bed brings a subtle change of shape and texture. The chocolate-brown bedspread contributes a welcome warm, dark tone among all the creams and oatmeals—a room composed entirely of pale naturals could be rather dull.

softly sophisticated

using chalky shades of pink in a cool, contemporary way

With its concrete floors and bare plaster walls, this cool modern space required a restrained contemporary look, but it was important that it did not become cold and impersonal. Using pink in a totally new way was an inspired decision, and the soft blossom sofa led the way. The shape is low and simple, contemporary yet comfortable. Upholstered in leather or dark wool, it would have dictated a completely different mood. Here, like a classic, beautifully tailored suit in an unexpected, true color, the effect of the pale pink is charming, immediately bringing a lightness of touch that is continued into the flowers and other details.

timeless natural textures

What more peaceful combination of colors to sleep surrounded by than shades of off-white and cream? Natural colors and textures come into their own in bedrooms, where you are aiming for a still, contemplative atmosphere without too many distractions. They are also a good way of pulling together a mix of different periods and styles, surfaces and textures. If your palette is restricted to a few shades, the colors and textures of different materials can be seen at their best: wood with its variety of tones and grains, rough or polished stone, shiny or matte metal, starched or soft-washed linen. Rather than fight against each other or get lost in a cacophony of clashing colors, each material has room to breathe and to work with the others to create an integral whole.

The natural harmony of this beautiful bedroom relies on a wide range of natural materials. The slightly rough texture of the time-worn stone at the windows and the warm, brown floorboards are part of the original architecture of the house. Added to this is the even richer dark brown of an antique chest of drawers, the gloriously organic shape and texture of Tom Dixon's raffia 'S' chair, some cool brushed metal in the form of lamps and tables, crisp white upholstery and bedlinen, and the pale blond wood of the contemporary bed itself. Too large an expanse of dark wooden floor can make even the sunniest room look gloomy; here, this is avoided with a pale rug that brings the illusion of light into the room.

When you are using neutrals, it's easy to get so caught up in the subtleties of tones and textures that you forget about pattern. But even in completely neutral tones, a beautiful print or pattern can add a glamorous softness to a room without disturbing the disciplined color palette. The drapes in this bedroom have a beautiful hydrangea pattern in white, dove gray, and silver. Bedlinen and upholstery are confined to the palest shades, with just the subtlest gold, silver, and gray printed detail on the bedcover.

"Different woods don't always blend well together. The pale new ash of this modern bed didn't seem right on the warm old floorboards until we added a plain neutral rug to ease the transition. The different tones and types of wood work as colors and textures in their own right but they need to be balanced with other elements in the room." TG

balancing old and new styles in a natural country bedroom

The juxtaposition of styles forces you to look at both in a new light. In this bedroom, the play of antique against modern creates an interesting dynamic: period architecture, wooden floorboards, a contemporary bed and chair, and an antique walnut chest of drawers in the corner. The surprise of this old chest alongside all the more up-to-date furniture really highlights the beauty of its warm color and patina. The contemporary ceramics and stylized flower arrangements placed on top maintain the playful tension right down to the details. And the drape fabric—an almost formal flower print with a fresh modern twist—pulls old and new together, creating a well-balanced and cohesive whole.

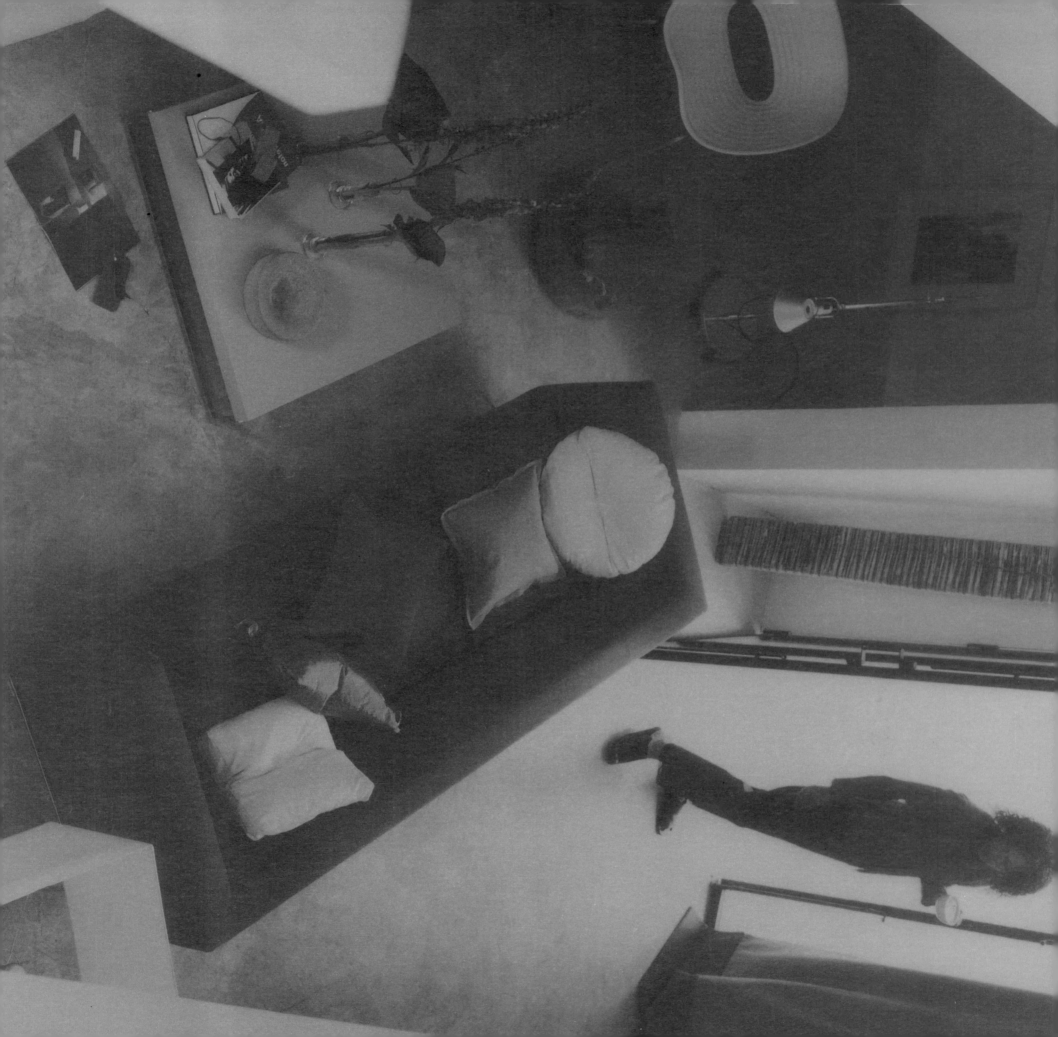

dynamic

sexy

persimmon

berry

rose

People are often frightened to use hot pinks and reds in a minimalist space, but warm colors can bring a real dynamism. The living room in this modern house in France is just such a cool, clean-cut space, but curvaceous furniture and rich voluptuous colors make it sexy and dynamic rather than cold and clinical. The use of colors, shapes, and textures that are warm and sensual but not overly feminine prevents the scheme from becoming too decorative. There are no patterns here, and the rich colors are countered by lots of white and neutrals. Although the overall impression is one of color, the vibrant shades are used only for the furnishings and textiles rather than on the walls, which are left white, or the floor, which is unadorned. This preserves the sense of perfect balance in the space. The mood could be changed again by painting a dynamic color on the wall.

The deepest color is concentrated in the cyclamen-mauve of the large three-seater sofa that defines the main seating area and in the full billowing drapes, in a lighter crocus shade with a thick border in the same shade as the sofa. The chair is pale clematis, and the pillows are white linen, clematis silk, and a wonderful persimmon, which seems to energize all the subtler pinks and mauves. Imagine the effect of taking that one persimmon pillow away—the whole mood would drop.

Not only are the colors voluptuous and sensual, the shapes are soft and curvy, too. Modern furniture is often thought of as linear and hard-edged, but the generous flowing shapes of the mauve sofa, white plastic chair, and clematis armchair illustrate the comfortable side of modernism. The soft shapes of the furniture indicate that some of the details can be more architectural; the square metal table and boxy lamp, for example, are more linear in form.

Textures have been chosen to warm up the overall scheme even more. The sofa is upholstered in the softest cashmere wool—also used at the windows to warm up the minimalist floor-to-ceiling panes. Crisp, white linen or leather might have been obvious choices for the upholstery, but the mood would have become too cool. The chair is covered in looped bouclé wool, which is comfortable but still very contemporary.

"In one sense, the scale is all wrong with these tall spindly foxgloves on a low table in a lofty white room. But they work—it is not just the color or their wayward curves, but also the sense that they are wild woodland flowers in this very contemporary setting. They offer an idea of eccentricity, which I love. It's also there in the one persimmon pillow—it's somehow amusing, eccentric, sexy. It says that you're not playing it safe." TG

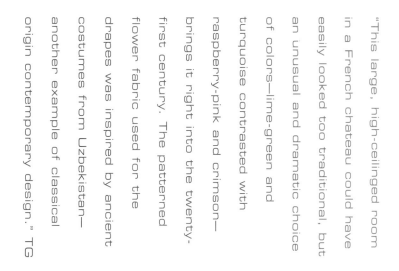

"This large, high-ceilinged room in a French chateau could have easily looked too traditional, but an unusual and dramatic choice of colors—lime-green and turquoise contrasted with raspberry-pink and crimson—brings it right into the twenty-first century. The patterned flower fabric used for the drapes was inspired by ancient costumes from Uzbekistan—another example of classical origin contemporary design." TG

brilliant color in an old French chateau

dazzling intensity

Lime-green and turquoise are seldom used in this way with raspberry-pink and crimson, but here the clean contrast is fresh and inviting, the greens and blues cooling down the heat of the rich berry shades. The beautiful bold flower print of the drapes takes the color right up to the soaring ceilings, and acts as a bridge between the traditional architecture of this French chateau, with its imposing windows, ornate detailing, and crystal chandelier, and the modern shapes and colors of the furnishings. The design of the print has a classic feel, but it has been given a modern twist and partnered with patterned borders and an inner panel of bright turquoise muslin.

Furniture has been confined to low, contemporary shapes—a long sofa in bright lime-green velvet, generously wide armchairs in pink and turquoise, and a square white table resting close to the ground. Contrary to expectations, long, low furniture looks great in a high room, adding to the sense of drama. The feeling of air and space in the room encourages further risks with color, placing a crimson peony-print panel on the lime sofa and a chartreuse pillow on a pink velvet chair. The peony-print has been echoed by real peonies arranged in vases on tables—their voluptuous, blowsy blooms are perfect for the grand, almost opulent feeling in this room. Again, their different intensities of pink are countered by the cool green of a curvaceous hosta leaf.

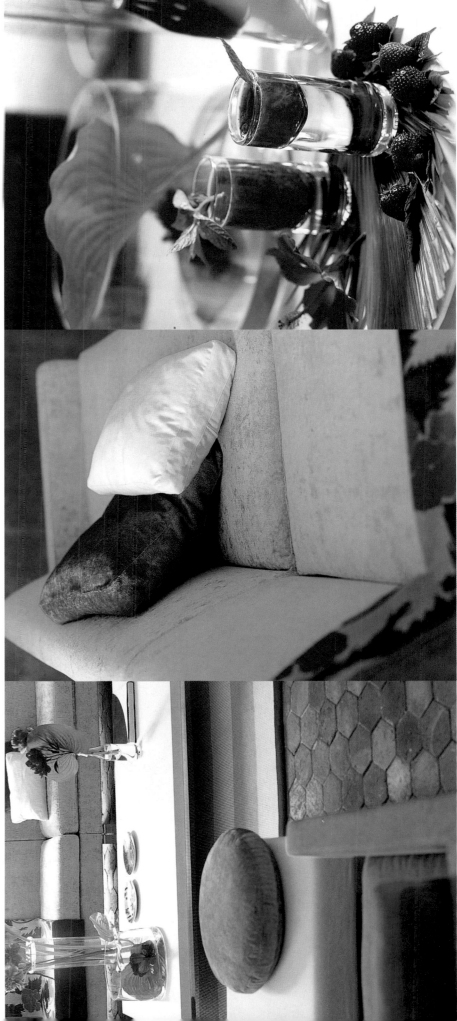

colors to make your heart sing

The table is laid in Tuscany for an impromptu early evening drink with friends. Slices of luscious watermelon look wonderful on a bright batik cloth with lots of little zinnia flowers, gathered from the garden and placed in individual glasses with a few leaves. It's a simple, spontaneous arrangement that catches the exact mood of the hour, as if the colors of a summer sunset have been drawn down onto the table—vibrant crimsons, reds, and oranges with just a hint of cooling green in the hosta, vine, and mint leaves.

"All the flowers on these pages were grown and gathered in my cutting garden. We grow poppies in all shades, from pale pink through scarlet and crimson to deepest purple-black, as well as zinnias, sweet peas, scented geraniums, and dahlias, and I'm constantly amazed by the way in which the rich beauty of their shapes and colors changes with the light. One of my greatest passions is choosing flowers and trying new combinations of colors and textures, hoping to create magic." TG

a sense of romance

Banners of shot silk in jewel-bright pink, red, and mauve are the only adornment at these elegant French windows. The rich colors glow with even more intensity with the sunlight shining through them and bathe the entire room in a soft, sensual glow. The mood is romantic without being overly feminine—indeed, the arrangement is almost minimal; with cooler colors and no pillows an entirely different atmosphere would be created. The clean lines of the modern daybed are covered in plain lilac bouclé wool and all the decorative detail is concentrated in the pillows—exquisite concoctions in embroidered silks, ikat weaves, and painterly florals that pick up on the principal colors.

soft, sultry opulence

Rich reds and pinks in bold prints and ikats create a warm and sultry mood in this beautiful French room. Ikat patterns have an exotic, opulent feel that conjures up the languid luxury of Middle-Eastern palaces; used here on a low modern daybed with piles of soft pillows all around, they bring a contemporary feeling to a traditional interior.

A room such as this, with its high ceilings and imposing architectural moldings, seems to demand a dramatic touch. The tall windows provide a great opportunity to use large patterns and to experiment with a succession of different layers of varying weights and textures. Lined printed linen, unlined silk brocade, and transparent muslin have been added like layers of paint on canvas to create a feeling of incredible richness. The drapes can be pulled across at different times of day and in various combinations to create a range of subtle and shimmering effects that change with the light and the seasons, altering the mood of the entire room.

This scheme manages to incorporate the whole spectrum of reds and pinks, from deep berry purples through scarlet and crimson to paler pinks and mauves. There is even a shot of bright persimmon in the pillows and on the broad cuff at the base of the drapes. Using all these shades together is a bold move that requires a sure hand. It works here because of the preponderance of neutrals in the existing architecture of the room. Surfaces are relatively unsophisticated, with subtly textured bare plaster walls and floors covered with hexagonal terracotta tiles. The raw pinkish materials act as a warm but neutral color in the room and help to balance the ikat weaves and textured silks, which may otherwise have felt almost oppressively opulent. Even the ikat patterns themselves have neutral shades printed or woven in with the richer colors, making them easy to use alongside other, more complex designs.

In spite of the rich mood, the furniture in the room is fundamentally simple. The design of the daybed is clean and minimalist, and the little bleached wooden table and the console fashioned from a slab of walnut fit perfectly into the scheme—their raw natural materials providing an earthiness that is welcome in such a grand room.

"This room is made for relaxing. The low shapes of the furniture, the ikat daybed with its piles of pillows, and the luxurious silk floor pillows all contribute to the sultry laid-back mood. The dominant horizontal shapes are countered by the long silk drapes, and the wide band of pure persimmon silk at the base of the drapes is a dynamic and interesting detail that links them back to other elements in the room." TG

layer upon layer of sensual silks and brocades

Warm neutral textures on the walls and floor make it possible to be bold with color and pattern. Mixing all tones of red and pink, from scarlet through crimson to candy, is not often done, but the shades used here are within the same essential color range, heated up by the odd touch of persimmon or deep berry, so the result is a harmonious combination. Feminine touches are confined to the details: the frill on a bolster, the pink silk ribbons on a pillow, and the pretty flower posies on shelves and tables.

"I've used all shades of red and pink in this room—pushing the combinations as far as they can go while maintaining the sultry, harmonious mood. Traditionally, such colors clash, but they all fall within the same sort of tonal family. Besides, what does clashing mean? The scheme works because of the warm neutrals in the raw plaster walls and tiled floors. All color and pattern is confined to the textiles, so why not experiment with lots of different patterns and textures? A room like this can take some eccentric touches." TG

vibrant contrasts

The grayish white plaster on the walls in this room demanded a fresher color scheme. The hot berry shades on the sofa are cooled down by the other colors in the room to create a lighter, more romantic mood. Notes of citrus and chartreuse cut through the sensual pinks and reds, and the flower arrangements are fresh and modern. The drapes are made from an ikat weave in fresh lavender, with layers of translucent silk behind and a cuff of bright lime green. Lots of white keeps the mood light and uplifting—white tables, sculptural lamps, and molded plastic chairs—with a large, round, white pillow adding a note of contrast on the sofa.

"Drapes are so often used too traditionally. I don't think you always have to match them in pairs—using panels or banners of different colors or patterns is a more modern way to bring interest to a room. The drapes here are in a lavender ikat weave with other panels in pale translucent silks. I've also used pattern in the rug—a vibrant voluptuous image in soft lavenders and grays that cools the pinkish ochre of the floor and helps to define the space." TG

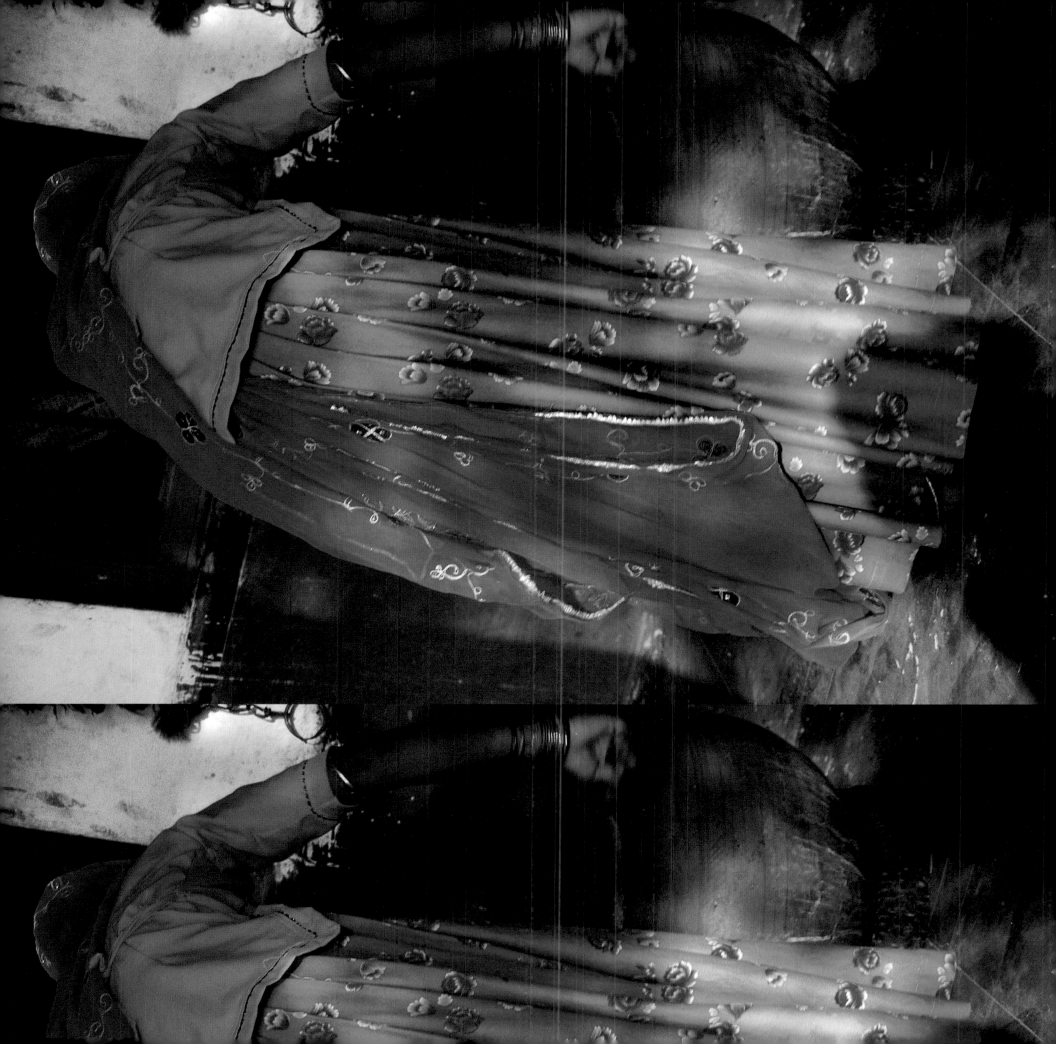

a touch of magic

Opening a kitchen cabinet can be as exciting as dipping into a box of paints, with as much potential for creativity. Think of every meal or party as a different picture, with the table as your blank canvas. Why use the same old placemats, plates, glasses, and table linens for every meal? Selecting and combining different tableware according to the occasion is a quick and easy way to alter the entire mood of a room, and it can be great fun, too. Mix and match various styles and colors to complement the food and the atmosphere. Either start with the food you want to serve and go with the colors and textures it suggests, or, for a special event, decide on the mood first and organize the food around it.

In many ways, serving food is as sensual and creative as decorating a room. The natural colors and textures of food are as inspiring as the finest silks and fabrics and their shapes as suggestive as sculpture. Picture the dark, glossy sheen of fresh cherries, the soft gleam of fish scales, the curvaceous contours of a cantaloupe. Plan your menu to look as good as it tastes, and create interesting contrasts in the accompanying salads and sauces. Plates, linen, and glasses can be chosen to complement the food, but keep the style simple and let your cooking do the work.

The modern approach to table decoration is to keep colors down to one or two shades, with maybe a contrasting accent color, and use placemats, cloths, or linen runners to make simple abstract patterns on the table. You don't need to do anything convoluted with napkins—crisp linen loosely folded is perfect. And the advantage of minimalist flower arrangements is that they take up less space on the table. Just scatter a few petals across the tablecloth or on a tray of desserts to add an air of casual romance.

Sometimes the simple beauty of fresh fruit, for example, is best left unadorned. But rather than just presenting it on a plate, try layering berries in different colors in a glass bowl with stripes of mint or basil leaves. Or bring a charming modern twist to a traditional recipe with an unusual container, such as the luscious panna cotta (opposite) served in painted Moroccan tea glasses.

"It's so important to create a sense of occasion, exciting the senses by presenting food in simple yet beautiful ways. Eating with friends should be a real celebration of all the senses—it is enriching to take the time to make a magical atmosphere, using flowers, leaves, and the food itself to set off all the delicious tastes and textures." TG

For this summer dinner party the dining-room table is given a bright new look with round felt mats in hot berry shades and vases of pink peonies, hyacinths, and guernsey lilies. Serving simple food in exotic and imaginative ways creates a light-hearted festive feeling. Here, fresh berries are suspended in fruit gelatin so that their colors make a pattern of stripes in clear glass tumblers. Clear ice buckets are lined with layers of strawberries, blueberries, cherries, and mint leaves and panna cotta is poured into painted tea glasses. The gelatins are decorated with blossoms and single petals are scattered around the food.

"The way food is served can be so visually exciting and individual—not about fussy ideas, just simple yet imaginative touches like serving panna cotta in these vibrant Moroccan glasses with rose petals bordering the plates in strips. Find inspiration in the contrasting colors and graphic shapes of the food itself, and from different glasses and ceramics." TG

relaxed

restful

lavender

blue

indigo

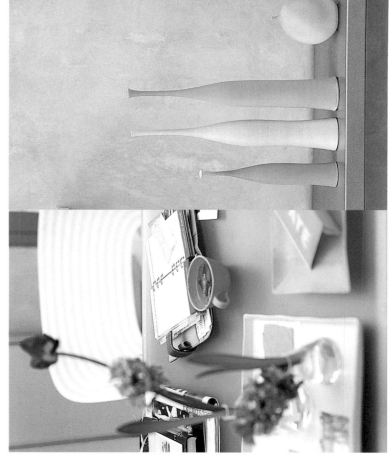

The quality of light coming through the slashes of glass in the roof gives this room the air of an artist's studio. One wall was formerly a strong cobalt blue, which dominated the mood and made for a dynamic, lively contrast with the books and ceramics collected on the shelves. The change of color to palest lavender on that wall and soft white plaster for the others has lowered the temperature and brought the room much more into line with its function as a study. The calmer colors make it feel much more like a working space, perfect for developing ideas or relaxing with a book. At the far end, a simple glass-topped table is used as a desk, but work in progress can be shut away in the modern metal cupboard behind it. In the middle of the room, low, molded, plastic chairs are grouped around the coffee-table—comfortable as well as elegant, they are upholstered in clear shades of linen.

The reorganization of the space allows it to work well as a private study, and it can easily be put to more sociable use. The conservatory is used more in summer, when the metal doors at the far end can be thrown open and a table and chairs taken out to the terrace overlooking the garden. In winter, space heaters prevent too much heat loss through the roof, while a rug may be added for extra warmth underfoot.

Along one wall, treasured ceramics and vases of flowers are arranged for their intrinsic beauty and the inspiration they provide. To pare down the space and calm the mood even more, the objects have been ruthlessly edited; the tableau of ceramics, books, and flowers is now as restful and inspiring as a still life by Giorgio Morandi. The objects can be changed from time to time to alter the atmosphere.

Reducing this room to its architectural elements and toning down the color has made it a more neutral space—a stage set in which the colors of flowers, books, and other favorite objects can create their own impromptu drama. Cutting out clutter can be extremely liberating, and it is claimed to improve concentration. The increased feeling of space also creates room for nature's own artistry—for the fleeting patterns of light and shade, and sun and cloud, to work their own subtle magic on the pale concrete floor and across the pale walls.

a romantic take on teatime in pale pastel colors

For a simple summer tea party in the conservatory, scoops of ice cream and wedges of chocolate cake are served in simple glass containers on a clean white background and scattered with just a few blossoms from a vase of pink hyacinths and tall white alliums. The gracious curve of a hosta leaf makes an impromptu mat, and sprigs of mint have been added to the refreshing herb tea, served from a clear modern-style teapot. Contemporary tableware and linen in a beautiful turquoise makes a good contrast to the sweeter pinks and mauves of the flowers.

"Nothing could be more luxuriant than the idea of an afternoon tea, in this case with the added indulgence of homemade ice cream and chocolate cake. The choice of plain, clear-glass containers, a cool white background, and touches of the palest mauves, pinks, and blues sets the scene. This is a new way of being romantic—the feeling is there but in a modern, minimalist style." TG

serene china blue

There is a wonderfully serene feel to this living room, with its high ceilings and pale gray plaster walls, and the quality of light from the windows is almost ethereal. Sometimes a single fabric provides the starting point for an entire color scheme. Here, the large-scale blue lily print used for the drapes has a strong, sophisticated feel that helps establish the mood of the room. Blue has a reputation as a cold color, but this is a warm shade with a certain amount of red in it. It's a bold choice, and the same china blue has been continued on the sofa and chair, and picked up in the delphiniums and hydrangeas in the flower arrangements.

This room is all about harmony rather than contrast, so the accent colors of magenta and soft pink were taken from the colors in the center of the blooms. These colors are picked up in the silk ribbon trim of the drapes, the pink linen chair, the patterns on the abstract rug, and in the simple vases of dahlias. There is also a lot of white, which complements the wonderful quality of the light. The restrained use of color, with an emphasis on subtle continuity between the different elements in the room, is what keeps the mood restful and relaxed.

Color, light, and texture work harmoniously together to create an atmosphere that is both restful and interesting, seductive yet cool. Textures range from the crisp starched linen of the drapes to a softer brushed linen on the sofa, chairs, and ottoman, and to the luxurious velvet for the pillows. A scheme such as this can be enhanced still further, even temporarily, by adding apparently clashing elements in the form of flowers and pillows in contrasting colors. The surprise of an orange pillow on a blue chair lifts the mood and adds a touch of dynamic energy. The room doesn't rely on this, but it illustrates the impact that just a few tiny touches of unexpected color can have.

"I've always been drawn to blues and mauves. I find these colors incredibly calming, but also quite sensual. The shade of blue in this room is warm—it has a lot of red in it—and it is warmed even more by the other colors with which it is mixed: magenta, crocus, orange, and the deep pink of a dahlia bloom." TG

tall blue flowers in an elegant setting

bold fabric echoed in a modern nature study

The large-scale blue-and-white fabric used for the drapes sets the tone of quiet sophistication in this stunning living room. The style and colors of the print are echoed in the multiple display of flowers on the modern console. The flower arrangements are romantic yet up-to-date, bringing a sense of lightness to the room that is relatively easy to achieve. Irises, delphiniums, and white peonies have been arranged in the same spirit of the lily print fabric—the individual blooms displayed in a row of glass vases like a modern botanical study.

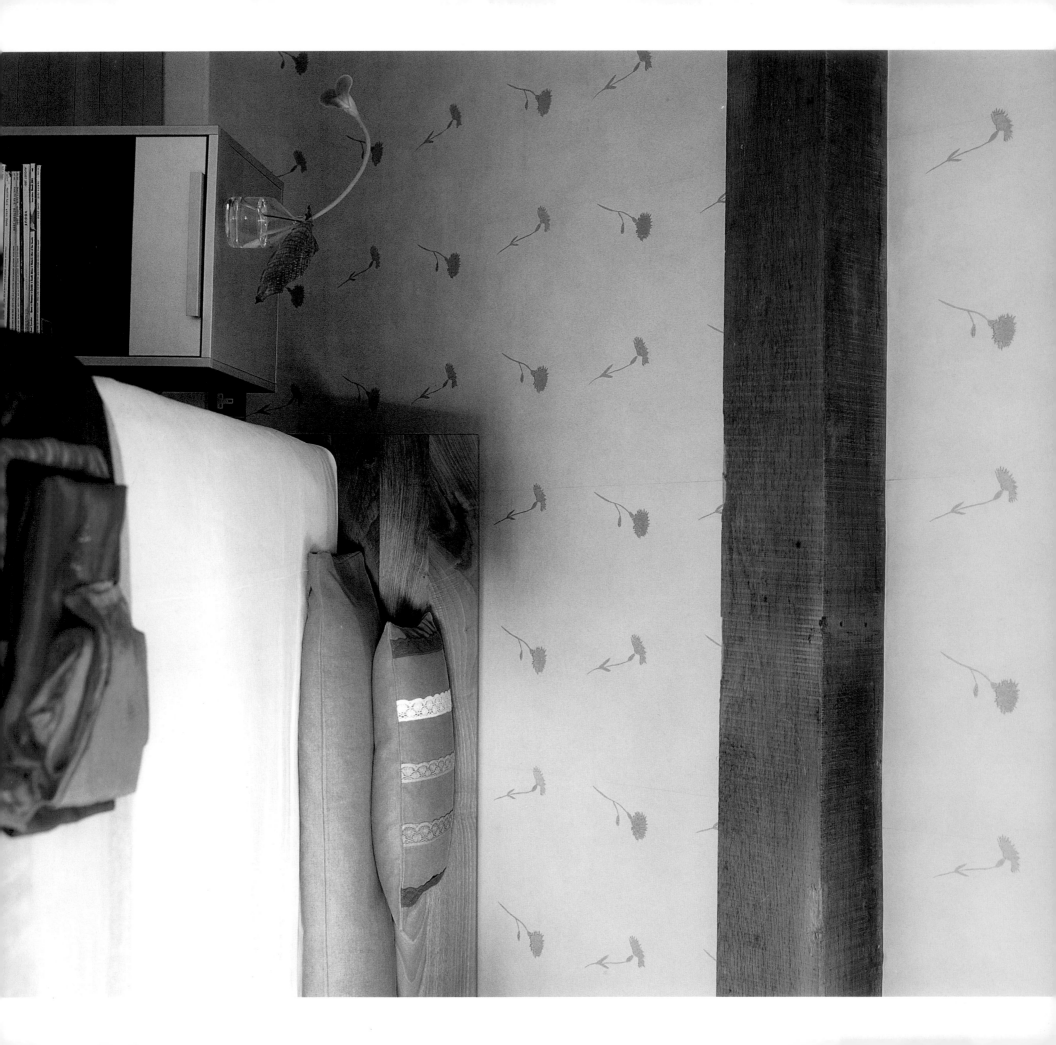

soft shades and charming patterns

This charming attic bedroom has been transformed through a creative combination of color and pattern. The sloping walls were a real challenge, and the unusual choice to paper them really paid off. A delightful sprigged cornflower print, which is repeated, slightly larger, at the windows, has exactly the right rustic credentials for a rural house, but is fresh and new rather than countrified. To emphasize the height in what could easily appear to be a poky space, the curtain pole has been hung as high as possible on the wall, with the fabric dropped in a long sweeping banner to the floor.

Confining the colors to one or two neighboring tones works well within a small room like this. Lavender and lilac are soft and pretty but still have a fresh contemporary edge. A clever use has been made of paint here—the far wall is a fresh clear shade of mauve, which helps unify the room, and the floorboards are painted a slightly lighter shade of the same color.

The old wooden beams have been left unpainted, however, to provide a reminder of the room's origins and to make a visual link with the new wood of the bed and other modern styles of furniture. The raw wood textures of the beautifully designed modern cabinet strikes just the right balance between rustic and modern, as do the hydrangeas on top of it. A winged armchair is another traditional classic, but this one has quirky, curly arms and is upholstered in crisp lilac linen. There is just a touch of contrasting color in the striped pillowcase and pink floral patterns on the bedcover. Otherwise, nothing disturbs the restful and relaxing atmosphere.

Paint can be an ideal way to breathe new life into potentially poky spaces. The narrow, twisting staircase leading up to this bedroom has been transformed with a coat of palest blue on the walls and a slightly darker shade on the stairs themselves, with fresh white for the baseboards and door frames. When wood—even old wood— is unremarkable or in bad condition, it often makes more sense to paint it than to strip and polish it. If it gets chipped or dirty, or you just want a change, repainting is easy.

"Look at the wonderful contrast between the gnarled old wood of the old beams and the smooth polished grain of this cabinet. The key to this attic room is taking traditional shapes and spaces and giving them a modern impression. Even these blue hydrangeas—the classic country garden flower—are modern when used with hosta leaves and a single purple calla lilly." TG

"When drawn, the banner of fabric at the window of this tiny bedroom can be admired like a painting, making a link with the flower-printed wallpaper. The floor-length swath of fabric also has the effect of making the window seem larger and the space more up-to-date and sophisticated—the metal curtain rail taken as high as possible to accentuate the length." TG

a contemporary outdoor room

relaxed comfort among the olive trees in an Italian country garden

Life spills out of the house into the garden in summer, and the square gravel terrace is as restful and relaxed as an indoor living room, providing a transition from the interior to the wilder garden beyond. The 'green architecture' has a graphic formality: the low box hedges act as walls to contain the space, while the clipped topiary cones and spheres are like living furniture or sculpture. Within this formal structure, the mood is spontaneous and relaxed, with chairs and small tables gathered in casual groups beneath the trees. Opening off to the side, in the shade of a simple pergola covered in vines, is a smaller, more enclosed space which is often used for dining.

"This farmhouse sits in a rural landscape, and the garden, with its orchard and olive trees, is quite rustic. I felt the need for a slightly more formal area near the house—this square of gravel with its box edging gives strong definition. The furniture is mainly light, modern, and relaxed, with lots of white plastic and metal, plus the rustic contemporary pieces, such as the bench of reclaimed wood." TG

classic calm blue and white

a delicate blossom print and shades of aquamarine

This little attic bedroom has been transformed into an airy modern space. Lots of pale blue has created a calm mood—the cherry blossom print on the walls has an Oriental feel, while pale paint on the floorboards reflects light from the window. Two single beds are covered in white linen, with throws and pillows that inject the only accents of stronger color—fresh limes and yellows with just a touch of clear pink. A curvy metal frame chair and metal table and cupboard create an attractive contrast with the original beams and old-fashioned latch door.

"We haven't been precious about original features in this attic room. It was a wise choice to paint the old floorboards and door—only the old ceiling beams have been left with their rough organic texture exposed. This preserves a sense of warmth and history in the room and adds to the exciting mix of old and now." TG

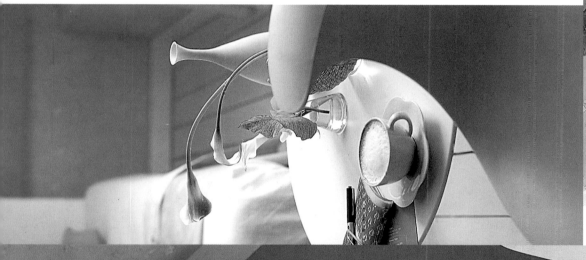

romantic and peaceful shades of mauve

restful lavender pink

The mood in this attic bedroom follows the architecture: romantic and verging on traditional but just a little quirky. The floral fabric at the window is quite formal, as is the use of patterned wallpaper, but there are just enough contemporary details to give the room a modern edge. The sleek metal bedside table, the cool gray and white ceramics, the banner of mauve and turquoise striped silk on the bed, and the idiosyncratic flower arrangements bring it right up-to-date. Flowers such as these are usually seen in great gaudy bunches—displaying them individually shows off each bloom for the miniature work of art that it is.

"This shade of lavender almost crosses over into pink—ideal for the romantic restful mood of this tiny attic bedroom. Large furniture can work in small rooms if they are kept uncluttered. Here, a big old-fashioned double bed almost fills the space, but simple shapes, light-colored fabrics, and lots of white bed linen make it feel bright and welcoming. The damask wallpaper gives a soft, subtle pattern and color. A tonal scheme in shades of mauve is gentle on the eye, with just one or two subtle accents of turquoise, red, and orange in the bedspread and flowers." TG

fresh

stimulating

turquoise

lime

leaf

This open-plan studio has separate areas for living and dining. The feeling is cool, and industrial, with modern metal-frame windows along one side, white walls, and a pale concrete floor, but the unexpected use of three colors—ocean blue, crocus, and just a touch of tangerine—gives it real warmth. These colors seem to instill vitality into the room, as do the simple silk curtains billowing in the breeze. Modern spaces often seem still and static, with their air-conditioning systems and fixed, closed windows, but here a sense of spontaneity seems to fill the room along with the fresh air. The mauve and orange on the furniture are separated in the subtle striped borders of the drapes, which were inspired by Indian saris. There is an interesting mixture of textures in the translucent silk window panels, the smooth, dry cotton of the sofa and ottoman, and the luxurious velvet on the chair and pillows.

The use of pattern on just one swivel chair is inspirational. It is surprising to find a floral print, with its traditional country associations, on such a modern piece of furniture. The print itself was inspired by an antique fabric from Uzbekistan, but has been given a contemporary spin with this bright orange-and-blue colorway. Orange is the key to the fresh and stimulating mood—the color works almost like an appetizer on the palate and gives the other colors a stronger edge. Without these touches of tangerine the room would have a much less invigorating atmosphere, since the other colors are really quite cool. Smaller orange details are woven through the space, like a bright thread in the flowers on the table and the mugs on the floor.

The design of the furniture follows the industrial feel of the architecture, the graphic lines giving the space an almost masculine feel, but unconventional colors and textures lend the room a lively sensuality. There is a careful balance between straight lines and curves—the clean-cut shapes of the sofa, ottoman, and orange chairs, and the sensual curves of the swivel chair and swirling abstract designs on the rug. The brushed-metal tables are an interesting combination of straight and curved lines, and hard and smooth surfaces. Even the flowers are in keeping with the theme—tall, white calla lilies in simple vases and a single orange hibiscus in a shallow concrete dish.

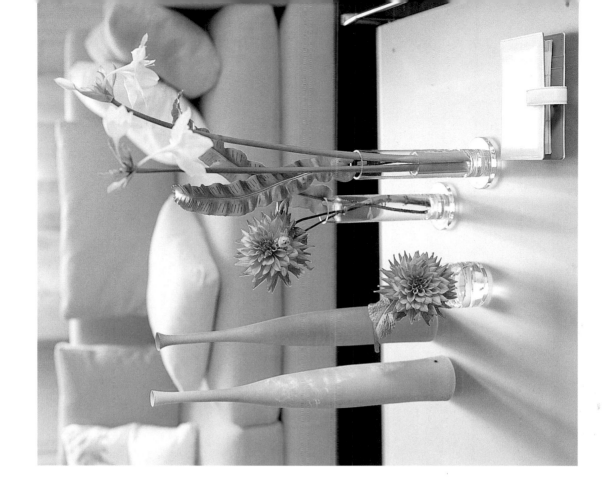

Blue is considered a peaceful, relaxing color, but this unusual mixture of bright turquoise and pale ocean with accents of lime and cantaloupe is fresh and stimulating. The architecture of this room in a French chateau is extremely formal, and its ornate paneled walls are painted a pale bluish gray (overleaf). To bring contemporary life and spirit to the room, a modern sofa upholstered in bright turquoise bouclé cotton leads the way, with lots of paler blues and white in the other furniture and details. The fabric at the window is a beautiful lily print, this time in turquoise on a crunchy white linen that looks almost translucent with the light shining through it. Under-curtains in a fine lace fabric with a leaf pattern add another layer of luminosity. The partnership of turquoise and lime is most successful—the lime directs the blue and white into a fresher, cooler combination, and is repeated in the chartreuse pillows and the color of the foliage in the vases of flowers. Meanwhile, the neutral base of the blue-gray walls is intensified in the pale blues and ocean colors used on the ottoman, throws, and pillows.

Subtly contrasting textures inject more interest: the bouclé cotton on the sofa, soft washed linen on the ottomans, and shiny white plastic for the smaller stools and tables. Most of the shapes lie long and low in this high-ceilinged space, but tall flower arrangements and the two elongated ceramic vases on the table provide a balance for all the horizontals. This is a strong, sophisticated look, the shapes of the furniture are pure and pared-down, the color palette and use of pattern restrained. For such a minimal style of decorating, however, the mood is unmistakably feminine. Pillows with pretty side bows and ribbon trims accentuate that feeling.

The look and feel of this room could easily be changed with the flowers and pillows alone. With only white flowers, the mood is cool and serene; the addition of a couple of perfect pinky orange dahlias and just one round cantaloupe pillow brings an element of surprise that's a real enlivener for the senses. Unexpected contrasts can heighten one's perception of graphic shapes and patterns—it is touches such as these that bring a real sense of warmth and comfort to the room.

"Who would think that just one pillow could be so important in the creation of a mood? This room would feel quite different without the cantaloupe orange pillow and the fiery orange dahlias on the table. Color used in this way is very flexible." TG

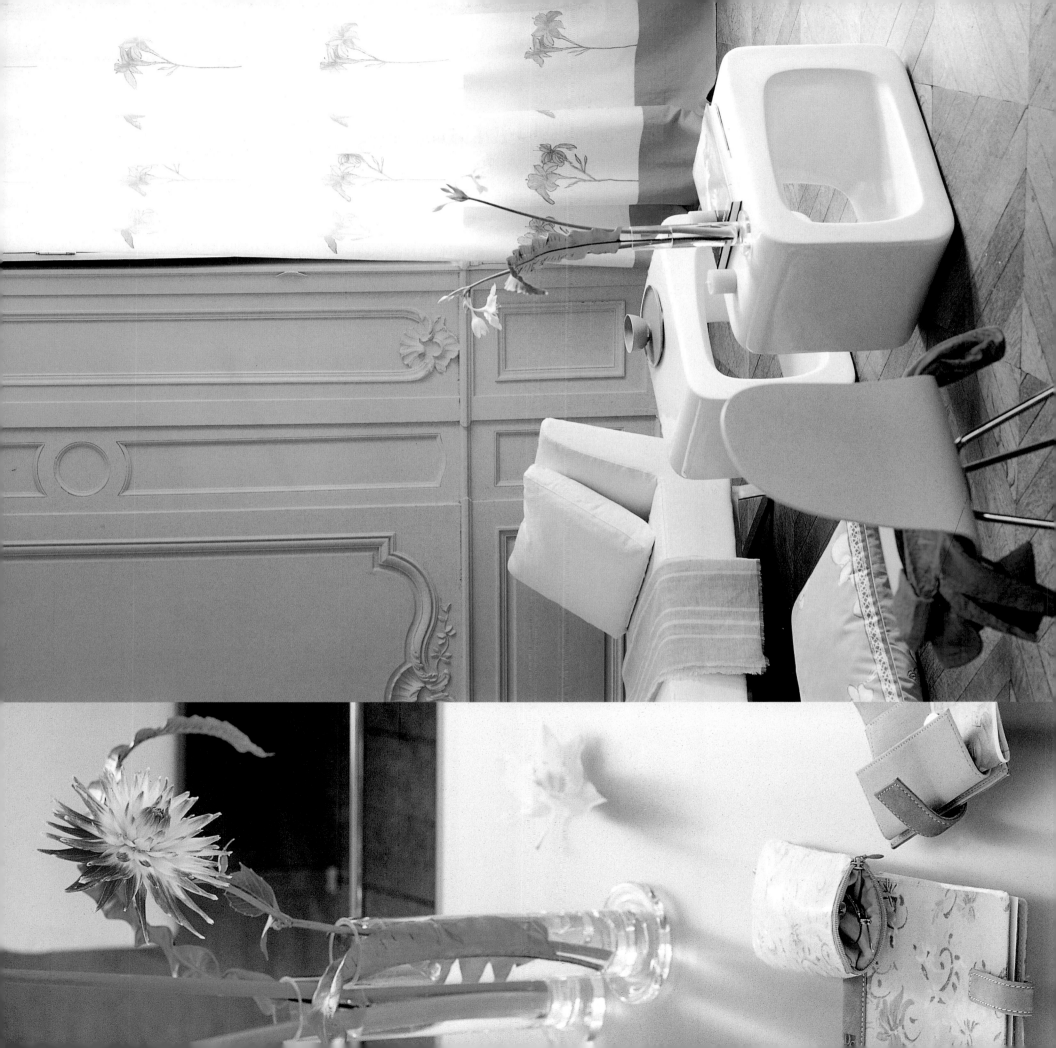

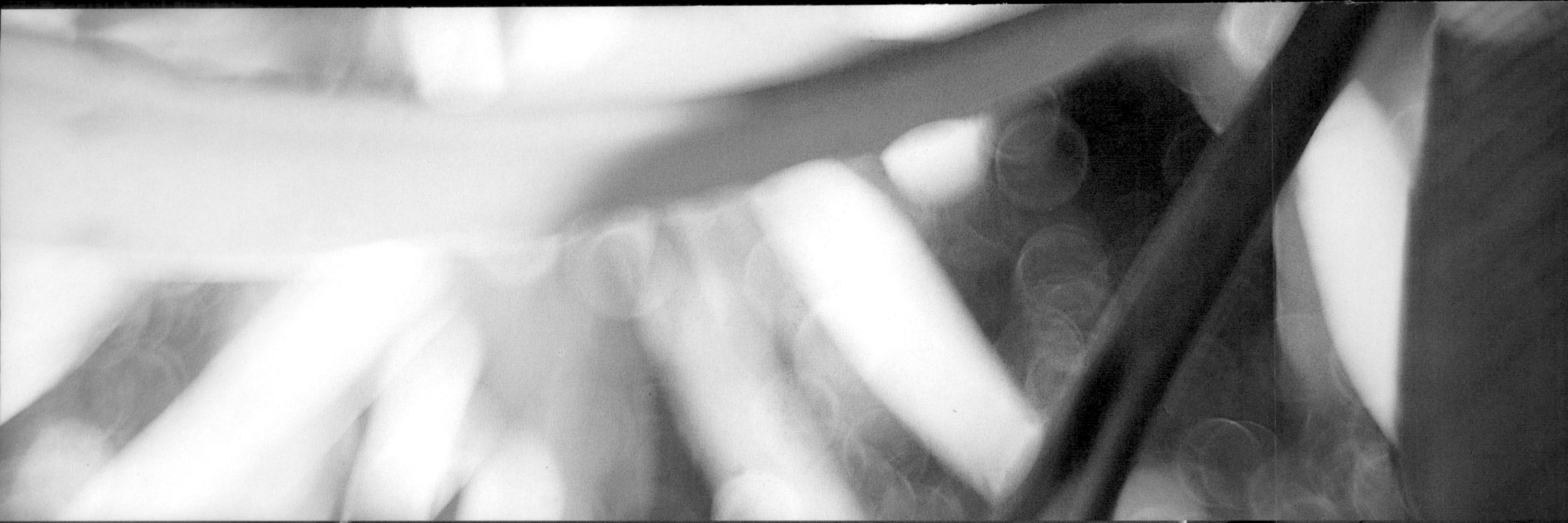

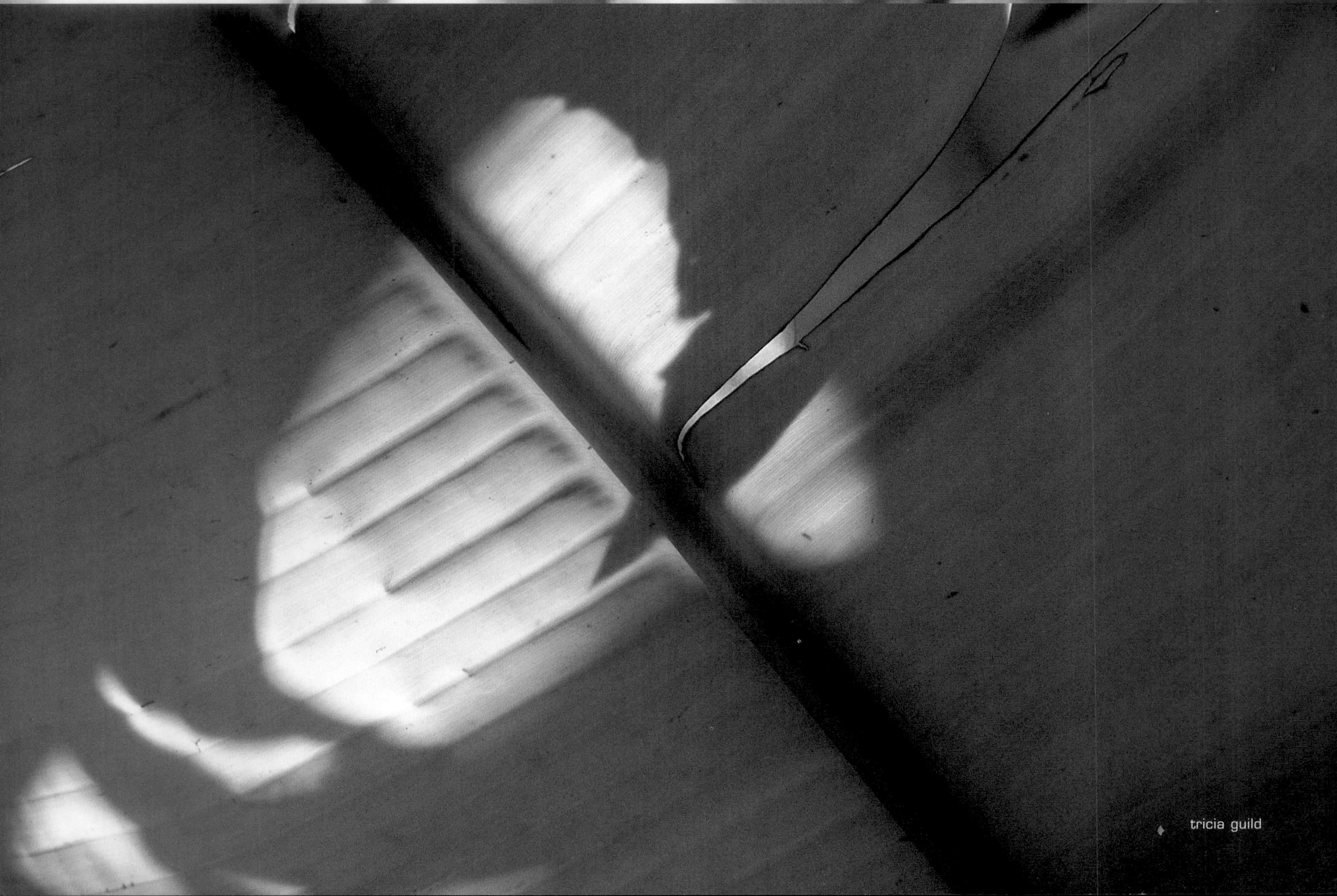

dymanic color and dazzling contrasts

A dazzling mixture of contrasting colors and patterns makes this hall a dynamic and welcoming space. A boldly patterned orange panel hangs at the tall windows, with wide cuffs of contrasting turquoise and under-curtains in chartreuse and turquoise checked muslin. The sofa is violet, the lamp a vibrant orange, and one armchair is upholstered in bright stripes that are offset with an equally colorful floral pillow. Everywhere you look there is richly concentrated color. Gazing into this room from another space is like looking into an exciting treasure chest—you can't wait to go in and explore.

The key to using such daring combinations is, as always, continuity. Often it is the colors of the larger elements in a room, such as a rug or sofa, which hold a room together. Here, it is the striped fabric used in various colorways on the armchair and pillows. All the colors in the room are to be found in these stripes—the chartreuse at the windows, the persimmon of the drapes, the rich mauve of the sofa—and even smaller accents, such as flowers, vases, throws, and pillows. This subtle color discipline, along with a conscious repetition of patterns in dynamic diagonals across the space, is what binds the seemingly disparate elements together and enables them to exist in harmony. Notice how the bold, metallic, stenciled fabric of the curtains is used again on the ottomans. The scheme may look free and spontaneous, but it only works because of the care and consideration behind it. The striped pillows have been placed with precision, and even flowers, vases, and books have been carefully chosen to knit into the scheme rather than disrupt its balance.

A neutral backdrop plays its part—this combination could not have been assembled in a space with strongly colored walls or floors. The creamy white walls and pale terracotta floors allow the colors to ring out in all their intensity, and there is a strong white presence in the plain armchair, the perfect counterbalance to its striped neighbor—the leather ottoman—and contemporary plastic tables. An expanse of the tiled floor is covered with a lighter material that also helps to increase the neutral component in the scheme. Anchoring all the elements is a large square white rug with turquoise and lime borders. This draws all the patterns, shapes, and tones together.

"You need a strong anchor to stabilize a daring combination like this. Without the white rug, these contrasting colors and patterns would have been floating in space, but the rug has the effect of drawing all the elements together onto their own island. This is what gives such a large empty space its atmosphere of intimacy. The stripes help blend it together, too, and give an exciting tension and mixture of graphic shapes." TG

places to sit in the sun and shade

in the heart of the garden

A walk around this leafy summer garden presents you with a choice of many different places to sit, from the furniture on the terrace near the house to the picturesque old bench and chairs in the shade of the cherry trees. Dip under the leafy arch and you're in the kitchen garden, where another table and stools have been placed in the sun. Nothing is fixed here—a table might be carried into the orchard for a summer lunch, or a bench moved to catch the last rays of the sun in the evening. Great fun can be had moving furniture around the garden and creating different scenarios—it's like picnicking with furniture.

"The garden is largely rustic and informal in feel, but the vegetable garden was designed along strong architectural lines, with the different vegetables and flowers confined to their allotted beds. The patterns created by neat rows of salad leaves, zucchini, and tomatoes are endlessly satisfying to look at, and clouds of bright flowers grow within separate squares, giving freedom to the geometric space." TG

the satisfying geometry of neat lines of crops

pleasures of picking and gathering for the table

Viewed from an upstairs window, the strong architectural design of the kitchen garden can be seen to full effect. There are four entrances, each with an arch entwined with clematis and wisteria, and intersecting paths divide the space into four principal squares. Within each square there are four more divisions, so the vegetables and flowers arranged in neat blocks and rows are like pieces of a living patchwork quilt. Pink and mauve flowers are concentrated on the side nearest the house, where pots of pink geraniums line the steps up from the terrace. On the far side, nasturtiums in every shade from deep red through orange to deep ochre and lemon romp among the vegetables with picturesque abandon. Wonderful large cactus-flowered dahlias are grown in the garden, in stunning shades of deep crimson, scarlet, orange, and pink.

This is a modern house in the country, and you can really feel the sunshine streaming into this space, with its bright citrus shades and leafy patterns. The predominant color is lime-green, accompanied by an interesting mix of turquoise, pale blues, fresh greens, and touches of pink. The hard lines of the architecture have been softened by the leaf print at the window—a reference to the trees outside, and the translucent checks in lime and turquoise filter the light and accentuate its sunny, dappled quality. The geometry of the square-paned windows is too strong to be ignored—it has been separated in the contemporary prints on the armchair, pillows, and ottoman.

"The colors here are harmonious and well balanced—adding another shade would break the spell. A chalky soft shade of pink on cushions, floor cushions, and in the ottoman print stimulates the other colors, rather than clashing with them. Lots of white prevents the scheme from cloying. Even the flowers—some luminous creamy dahlias from the garden—are almost exclusively white." TG

"I took the lead for this scheme from the long stylized flowers embroidered on the border of the tablecloth. They have a wonderfully graphic quality, with a modern edge that is accentuated by the matte ceramic plates and tall, elegant glasses. Even the lemon cake, cut into long, thin wedges, makes a real impact on the pale blue handmade plates." TG

grapefruit cocktails, an appliqué tablecloth, and slices of fragrant lemon tart

Simple indulgences can be just as enjoyable as more elaborately planned meals—sometimes more so. This table has been set with a pretty appliqué cloth and pale blue handmade ceramics, and just a few dahlia blooms floated in little cups or scattered onto plates. A fresh lemon tart is drizzled with lemon syrup and cut into slim slices. Champagne mixed with grapefruit and mango juice in pretty antique glasses is the perfect accompaniment, with the sun shining through the fluted glass. The mood is uplifting, with the scent of lemons hanging in the air.

Designers Guild fabric and wallpaper directory

All upholstered furniture by Designers Guild unless otherwise stated.

page 12

Wide Square chairs in Brera Chalk
F562/15 and Marianao Persimmon
F1030/04

Curtains in Ribailagua Natural F1033/01

Voiles in Habanera Acacia F1046/03

Wallpaper in Marianao Persimmon
P378/05

Striped cushions in Lucetas Leaf F1049/02

page 18

Wide Square Chairs in Nurata Ocean
F1021/14 and in Nurata Geranium
F1021/09

Edge Stool in Nurata Mango F1021/11

Curtains in Zekh Peony F1013/04 with
binding in Makasar Acacia F970/09

Voiles in Cozenza Peony F1015/04

Floor cushion in Alacha Crocus F1008/03

page 20

Scoop Sofa in Coba Leaf F1005/08

Curtains in Brera Lapis F562/43 and in
Brera Chalk F562/15

page 22

Chill Sofa in Brera Cantaloupe F562/44

Box Chairs in Brera Chartreuse F562/41
and in Brera Cantaloupe F562/44

Scoop Chair in Brera Chalk F562/15

Chill Stools in Brera Marine F562/40 and
in Brera Chalk F562/15

Curtains in Brera Crocus F562/46 and in
Brera Chalk F562/15

Page 30

Square Sofas in Lucetas Crocus F1049/04
with seat cushion in Brera Crocus
F562/46 and in Lucetas Peony
F1049/03 with seat cushion in Brera
Lapis F562/43

Edge Stool in Marianao Ocean F1030/03

Throws on seat cushion in Vitrales Violet
F1032/03 and in Habanera Aqua
F1046/02

Curtains in Santovenia Peony F1027/02

Page 33

Sleep Sofa in Izapa Magenta F993/02

Scoop Chair in Brera Peony F562/45

Box Chairs in Brera Cantaloupe F562/4
and in Caracol Peony F997/03

Floor Cushions in Pontalba Cyclamen
F980/O, in Edzna Magenta F996/02
and in Tikal Persimmon F994/05

Curtains in Cabildo Schiaparelli F985/02

Voiles in Reticella Persimmon F1000/02
and in Estrella Cerise F999/02

Rug in Barrisdale Ecru

Page 35

Tight Sofa by B&B Italia in Fiesole Clematis
F968/05

Apta Chair by B&B Italia in Brera Chalk
F562/15

Striped cushion in Lucetas Crocus
F1049/04

Voiles in Bise White F942/01

Doors painted in TG Blue

Page 38

Elan Sofa by Cappelini in Brera Chalk
F562/15

Solo Chair by B&B Italia in Fiesole Clematis
F968/05

Floor cushion in Alacha Peony F1008/01

Voiles in Bise White F942/01

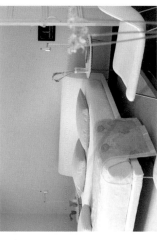

Page 49

Spider Sofa by Cappelini in Brera Chalk
F562/15

Upholstered cubes in Brera Blossom
F562/26 and in Brera Chalk F562/15

Page 54

Glide Chair by Cappelini in Parioli Verdigris
F969/07

Floor Cushion in Parioli Aquamarine
F969/08

Cushions in Parioli Chartreuse F969/09
and in Khiva Chartreuse F1020/06

Page 64

Loop Daybed by Cappelini in Brera Blossom
F562/26

Curtain in Simoon Petal F938/08

Curtain on bed in Bise White F942/01

Bedcover in Brera Chalk F562/15

Pillows in Brera Blossom F562/26

Throw on bed in Timbalier Blossom
F918/06

Rug in Barrisdale Ecru

Page 59

Bed and bedcover in Brera Chalk F562/15

Curtains in Carriaco Ice F921/07

Spring Chaise by Cappelini in Brera Chalk
F562/15

Throw on bed in Chandeleur Aqua F917/02

Pillows in Brera Marine F562/40

Rug in Barrisdale Ecru

Page 58

Elan Sofa by Cappelini in Brera Ocean
F562/39

Curtains in Brera Chalk F562/15 with
binding in Brera Marine F562/40

Page 77

Solo Sofa by B&B Italia in Safed Silver
F905/01

Rockford Chair in Gabanti Granite
F904/03

Curtains in Timurid Steel F893/04

Cushions in Brera Chalk F562/15, in
Canareggio Pewter F907/16 and in
Trovaso Sky F906/05

Page 70

Spider Sofa by Cappelini in Brera Water
Blue F562/18

Curtains in Callan Natural F619/02

Page 79

Bedcover in Safed Peat F905/03

Square pillows in Safed Oatmeal F905/04

Throw on bed in Nakshe Natural F897/05

Curtains in Safed Oatmeal F905/04

Voiles in Batiste Natural F882/01

Page 80

Elan Sofa by Cappelini in Brera Blossom
F562/26

Solo Chair by B&B Italia in Brera Shell
F562/27

Curtains in Simoon Petal F938/08

Floor cushions in Brera Shell F562/27, in
Brera Chalk F562/15 and in Brera
Crocus F562/46

Page 85

Charles Chair by B&B Italia in Trovaso Pearl
F906/01

Bedcover in Brera Chalk F562/15

Throw in Carriaco Silver F921/02

Curtains in Chandeleur Pearl F917/04

Rug in Barrisdale Ecru

Page 90

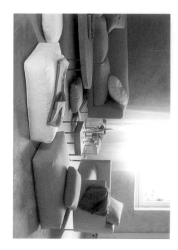

Elan Sofa by Cappelini in Fiesole Cyclamen

Edge Chair in Nurata Geranium F1021/09

Curtains in Paranja Leaf F1014/01 with
binding in Sulu Poppy F973/04

Throw in Alacha Peony F1008/01

Rug in Morriston Putty with bindings in
Rouge and Ocean

Page 92

Edge Sofa in Nurata Leaf F1021/12

Glide Chair by Cappelini in Parioli Orchid
F969/03

Curtains in Fiesole Clematis F968/05 with
binding in Fiesole Cyclamen F968/04

Cushions in Fiesole Persimmon F968/01
and in Makasar Pale Cyclamen F970/10

Page 98

Loop Daybed by Cappelini in Parioli Bluebell
F969/06

Curtains in Makasar Peony F970/03 and in
Sulu Clematis F973/05

Page 101

Wisconsin Daybed in Sabai Cerise
F974/01

Spider Chair by Cappelini in Fiesole
Persimmon F968/01

Curtains in Puca Damson F960/03 with
binding in Celebes Geranium F972/06
and in Makasar Peony F970/03

Page 104

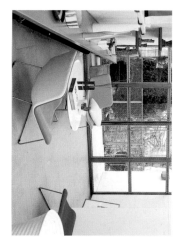

Escape Sofa in Khiva Cassis F1020/04

Box Chairs in Nurata Peony F1021/08 and
in Nurata Chartreuse F1021/13

Edge Stool in Khiva Chalk F1020/14

Curtains in Nilobi Hyacinth F1011/03 with
binding in Makasar Acacia F970/09

Voiles in Cozenza Hyacinth F1015/03

Page 116

Spring Chairs by Cappelini in Brera Lapis
F562/43, in Brera Cantaloupe
F562/44 and in
Brera Mauve F562/04

Page 123

Square Sofa in Mahe Hyacinth F466/08

Edge Stool in Khiva Chalk F1020/14

Square Chair in Brera Cyclamen F562/22

Curtains in Pontalba Hyacinth F980/02

with binding in Sulu Clematis F973/05

Voiles in Cozenza Hyacinth F1015/03

Page 128

Maroushka Metz Chair in Brera Crocus

    F562/46

Curtains in Pitot Lilac F986/03

Bed covered in Brera Chalk F562/15

Throw in Courcelle Lilac F979/01

Walls papered in Pitot Lavender P354/03

Page 135

Curtains in Mistral Leaf F939/03

Throw in Carondulet Ocean F983/02

Bedcover in Brera Chalk F562/15

Pillows in Brera Marine F562/40

Floor painted in Cloud

Walls papered in Sakura Turquoise

    P305/01

Page 136

Curtains in La Dcsirade Lilac F920/02

Bedcover in Brera Chalk F562/15

Throw on bed in Torsello Magenta

    F879/03

Walls papered in Beausejour Lilac

    P323/03

Page 144

Scoop sofa in Khiva Ocean F1020/08

Scoop chair in Nurata Mango F1021/11

Chill Stool in Khiva Crocus F1020/11

Sunset Chair by Cappelini in Paranja Cobalt

    F1014/04

Curtains in Rucellai Crocus F1019/05

Page 148

Chill Sofa in Coba Marine F1005/05

Chill Stools in Brera Marine F562/40 and

    in Brera Chalk F562/15

Curtains in Pontalba Azure F980/03 with

    binding in Brera Marine F562/40

Voiles in Merletto Ocean F998/04 and

    Merletto Leaf F998/06

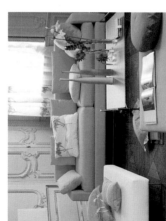

Page 157

Edge Sofa in Tejeda Mauve F1048/04

Edge Chairs in Tejeda Chalk F1048/07 and

    in Alfarjes Leaf F1050/01

Edge Stools in Corazon Chartreuse F1031/05

    and in Corazon Ocean F1031/06

Curtains in Corazon Persimmon F1031/02

    with binding in Corazon Ocean F1031/06

Voiles in Yambu Lime F1047/01, Yambu

    Ocean F1047/02, Habanera Aqua

    F1046/02 and Habanera Acacia

    F1046/03

Page 162

Chill sofa in Tejeda Lime F1048/18

Wide Square Chair in Brera Chalk

    F562/15 with seat cushion in Vitrales

    Blossom F1032/01

Edge Stool in Ribailagua Ocean F1033/03

Curtains in Amarillo Marino F1028/01

Voiles in Yambu Ocean F1047/02 and in

    Yambu Lime F1047/01

Floor Cushion in Vitrales Blossom

    F1032/01

Designers Guild stockists

Designers Guild fabrics and wallpapers are distributed in the US and Canada by

Designers Guild lifestyle is available from the Designers Guild store at 267-277 Kings Road, London SW3 5EN

Designers Guild products are available in over 40 countries, including the following:

USA

Chicago
Osborne & Little Inc
Merchandise Mart – Suite 610
Chicago IL 60654
Tel: (312) 467-0913
Suite 304
Denver CO 80209
Tel: (303) 778-7088
Fax: (303) 778-7489

Denver
Shanahan Collection
Denver Design Center
595 S. Broadway
Suite 100-S

Cleveland
Gregory Alonso Showroom
Ohio Design Center
23533 Mercantile Road
Suite 113
Beachwood OH 44122
Tel: (216) 765-1810
Fax: (216) 765-1858

Philadelphia
JW Showroom, Inc.
The Marketplace
2400 Market Street
Suite 304
Philadelphia PA 19103
Tel: (215) 561-2270
Fax: (215) 561-2273

Minneapolis
Gene Smiley Showroom
International Market Square
275 Market St. – Suite 321
Minneapolis, MN 55405
Tel: (612) 332-0402
Fax: (612) 332-0433

San Francisco
Osborne & Little, Inc.
101 Henry Adams Street
Suite 435
San Francisco CA 94103
Tel: (415) 255-8987
Fax: (415) 255-8985

Osborne & Little Inc
90 Commerce Road
Stamford CT 06902
Tel: (203) 359-1500
Fax: (203) 353-0854

New York
Osborne & Little Inc
979 Third Avenue-Suite 520
New York NY 10022
Tel: (212) 751-3333
Fax: (212) 752-6027

Boston
The Martin Group Inc
One Design Center Place
Suite 514
Boston MA 02210
Tel: (617) 951-2526
Fax: (617) 951-0044

Florida
Design West Inc – DCOTA
1855 Griffin Road – Suite A474
Dania Beach FL 33004
Tel: (954) 925-8225/8226/8227
Fax: (954) 922-8748

Atlanta
Ainsworth Noah & Assocs
1700 Stutz Drive – Suite 60
Troy MI 48084
Tel: (248) 643-8828
Fax: (248) 649-2366

Rozmallin
Atlanta GA 30324-1325
PO Box 14325
Tel: (404) 231-8787
Fax: (404) 233-5418

Los Angeles
Osborne & Little Inc
Pacific Design Center
Suite B643
8687 Melrose Avenue
Los Angeles CA 90069
Tel: (310) 659-7667
Fax: (310) 659-7677

Dallas
ID Collection
1025 North Stemmons
Freeway – Suite 745
Dallas TX 75207
Tel: (214) 698-0226
Fax: (214) 698-8650

Houston
ID Collection
5120 Woodway – Suite 4001
Houston TX 77056
Tel: (713) 623-2344
Fax: (713) 623-2105

Oakmont
Pacific Design Center
Suite B647
8687 Melrose Avenue
Los Angeles CA 90069
Tel: (310) 659-1423
Fax: (310) 659-7332

Washington DC
Osborne & Little Inc
300 D Street SW – Suite 435
Washington DC 20024
Tel: (202) 554-8800
Fax: (202) 554-8808

Seattle
The Joan Lockwood
Collection, Inc.
5701 6th Ave S – #203
Seattle, WA 98108
Tel: (206) 763-1912
Fax: (206) 763-3072

Canada
Primavera
160 Pears Ave – Ste. 110
Toronto Ontario M5R 3P8
Canada
Tel: (416) 921-3334
Fax: (416) 921-3227

South America

Argentina
Mrs Miranda Green
Cabello 3919
1425 Buenos Aires
+54 1 802 0850

Brazil
Formatex Representacoes Ltda
Rue Oscar Freire, 1119
Sao Paulo, CEP 01426-001
Brazil
+11 38 97 8130

Chile
Les Tissus
Nueva Costanera 3730
Vitacura Santiago
+56 2 246 5665

Columbia
Denise Webb & Associates
Diseño Interior
Calle 79b # 7-59 Int. 4a
Bogotá Columbia
+571 255 6194

Curaço
The Jungle
Lindberghweg #1
+59 99 465 8640

Mexico
Artell Sa de CV
Calle 20 No 9
Colonia San Pedro
De Los Pinos
Mexico 03800 Df
+52 5 272 2861

Aruba
Terra Nostra
Decorations NV
Caya GF Croes 2
PO Box 5080, Oranjestad
+297 8 30312

Australia
Designers Guild Fabric & Wallpaper (Australia)
60 Corporate Drive
Moorabbin Victoria 3189
+61 3 9552 6000

Linen House (bed & bath)
Level 1
79-81 Frenchmans Road
Randwick NSW 2031
+61 2 9326 5111

Austria
Victoria Schoeller-Szüts
Boersengasse 9/10
A-1010 Wien
+43 1 535 3075

Belgium & Luxembourg
Acanthus Interiors Sprl
J.Eerdekensstraat 27
B-3001 Heverlee
+321 6 292 316

Bermuda
Howe Enterprising
PO Box Hm 3222
Hamilton Hmpx
+1 441 292 1433

Cyprus
L.I.Christofides
PO Box 1310
9 Loukis Akritas Ave
Nicosia
+357 2 772 939

Denmark
LG Décor (fabric & wallpaper)
Vejenbrødvej
3 Avderød
Dk-2980 Kokkedal
+45 48 28 16 06